TALES FROM THE

DAVENPORT

Mick — Thank you!
Larry Strickland

LARRY STRICKLAND

P.106

TALES FROM THE
DAVENPORT

Second Printing 2011

Illustrated by: Evan Bailey

ISBN: 0-9728872-8-8

Published and printed by Trent's Prints
Chumuckla, Florida
866.275.7124
www.trentsprints.com

dav*en*port (noun): sofa or couch

TALES FROM THE
DAVENPORT

Second Printing 2011

Illustrated by: Evan Bailey

ISBN: 0-9728872-8-8

Published and printed by Trent's Prints
Chumuckla, Florida
866.275.7124
www.trentsprints.com

dav*en*port (noun): sofa or couch

We have a weight to carry,
and a distance we must go.
We have a weight to carry,
a destination we can't know.
We have a weight to carry,
and can put it down no where.
We are the weight we carry,
from there to here to there.

---Dean Koontz
The Book of Counted Sorrows

Dedicated to

Mom, Dad, my brother Greg, my sister Terri, and my children: Gabriel, Megan, and Tisha

Forward by the Author

This book was a four year project that caused me to relive a lot of good times, bad times, and sad times. My oldest daughter Megan contributed so much. She transcribed my dictations and helped me with wording and structure. Without her help, this book would not have been possible. There were times when we would argue and times when we would laugh. All my love to her. **Be forewarned readers** that this book does contain adult language and content! For parents of younger children, let them grow up first before reading. And then again, there are some stories that you should share with them that would help them on their way to maturity. Read and enjoy!

Larry Strickland
A.k.a. Strick 9

A Special Thanks To:

Evan Bailey
Book Cover and Illustrations

Evan is a true, gifted artist who I enjoyed working with.

To contact this artist:

Evan Bailey

Email: RawPower455sd@hotmail.com

REVIEWS

"Though 'Tales From The Davenport' contains enough warped rock episodes to warrant Larry a spot on VH1's 'Behind The Music', a surprising element of the book is its warmth. Sure, I loved the sicko peanut butter episode and all the wild gig stories, but Larry's soul shines through with tales of friends, family and others who have touched his life. Definitely, a fun summer read. But would be rockers be warned: Don't try ANY of this at home."
                                    -Troy Moon/Pensacola News Journal

"A hilarious collection of short stories, 'Tales From The Davenport' takes you along on the bumpy ride of a musician's life and gives you the PG-13, and sometimes R-rated preview of what life as a rock star is really like. Oh, and it touches on some lessons Larry learned as a kid too, like don't lick the ice tray. This book is amusing, shocking and touching all at once."
                                    -Tiffany Napper/Editor for The Pelican

"Since it covers subjects ranging from his grandfather's love for Canned Heat to his case of piano neck to living for three weeks on frog legs, I think it is safe to say that Larry has written a book unlike any most of us have ever read."
                                    -Fran Thompson/Mullet Wrapper

"I found the book, 'Tales From The Davenport' quite entertaining and funny and is an interesting look at a very Talented Musicians life."
                                    -Phil Thomas Katt/UZ-TV

"Flora-Bama's own Larry Strickland has added one more item to his resume'- author... This is a great beach read with short descriptive stories, and illustrations... A family affair to be sure... Larry's life is a must read full of life's lessons learned, forgotten, and learned again."
                                    -Pat McAuliffe/The L.A.Bull

Table of Contents

The Lesson   Page 1

       Illustration 1   Page 3

Devil In The Window   Page 5

IceTray   Page 7

My First Fish   Page 9

Hard Times   Page 11

Baptism By Fire   Page 13

The First Acting Role   Page 15

The Beginning Of Music   Page 17

The First Drink   Page 21

       Illustration 2   Page 23

Eat A Peach   Page 25

Running To Practice   Page 27

First Time Stoned   Page 29

First Surfing Experience   Page 31

Canned Heat   Page 33

First Time Busted   Page 35

       Illustration 3   Page 37

The Pill Bottle   Page 39

The Banana Story   Page 41

Snort Bombs   Page 43

Frog Legs   Page 45

The Dead Wagon   Page 47

Intendencia Street   Page 49

Mushrooms and Peanut Butter   Page 51

Illustration 4   Page 53

The Night I Died   Page 55

The Red Devil Tornado Story   Page 57

The Pass   Page 61

Illustration 5   Page 63

Almost Famous   Page 65

Going To California   Page 67

The Smoking Helmet   Page 71

Illustration 6   Page 73

The Procol Harum Story   Page 75

The Spitting Story   Page 77

Memphis   Page 79

Piano Neck   Page 81

Chitterlings   Page 83

Marriage Number One   Page 85

Steeple Jack Man   Page 87

Lounge Lizard   Page 89

The Strangest Thing   Page 91

The Prince of Darkness   Page 93

My First Record   Page 95

Second Marriage   Page 97

Commode   Page 99

Magic   Page 101

Rolling Death Trap   Page 103

The M&M Peanut   Page 105

Illustration 7   Page 107

Scott Free   Page 109

Dave Mason   Page 111

Shark Encounter   Page 113
    Illustration 8   Page 115
Skunk and Snake   Page 117
Stuff This   Page 119
Strick 9   Page 121
Flora-Bama Story   Page 123
    Illustration 9   Page 131

Poems and Lyrics   Page 133
    Baylen Street   Page 135
    Begin To Begin   Page 137
    The Flag Fell In Atmore   Page 139
    Thoughts   Page 141
    Mean Ole' Woman Blues   Page 143
    Whiskey's My Companion   Page 145
    Movin' On   Page 147
    Crossover   Page 149

Philosophical Sayings & Definitions   Page 151
    Philosophical Sayings   Page 153
    Definitions   Page 155

Hiccups   Page 157
A Membranth   Page 159
Acknowledgments   Page 161

THE LESSON

The sound of war cries filled the air. Throwing down the shovel that I was using to bury my dead goldfish, I reached for my trusty six-shooter and rolled behind a bush.

Coming up in a crouch, I started firing off round after round. To my satisfaction I managed to eliminate all foes. Leaning back, I breathed a sigh of relief. Now I could get back to the task at hand. Laying to rest my favorite goldfish was not an easy thing for a boy of four to do.

How long had I been in this wilderness? Oh, how long was I to suffer?

Suddenly, I felt a need so strong as to not be denied. A feeling, that you as a reader, I'm sure has had before.

As I looked around in vain for a way out of the trap that I had let ensnare me, I realized that it was fruitless to deny my destiny. So be-it, let the Gods of fate control me.

Now was the time! Now was the hour of my need! When I had been fighting the heathens that attacked me, when I had been grieving for my lost pet, Mother Nature had crept up on me.

There was no way out! The urge was too strong! Ah relief, ah sweet bliss! I had defecated in my shorts! Now what was I to do? Only one thing to do, run to the house, run to the bathroom and rid myself of this foul load. Taking off my shorts, I threw my underwear into the corner. Putting my shorts back on, out of the house I ran.

1

Continuing my quest, I had no idea what awaited me.

From the land of reality came the cry "Larry, come home!"

As I raced back, I had no idea what fate stood in store for me. The old woman that took care of me said, "Look, I made some homemade peanut-butter just for you!" Oh how my heart thrilled at the thought of such a wonderful treat!

And now she puts her hand out with a small portion of the creamiest looking peanut butter these small eyes had ever seen. "Larry, put your finger in and get yourself a big taste."

I slowly stuck my finger in and scooped out a large portion. Slowly drawing it to my mouth, I closed my eyes in anticipation.

Injecting this lump of what I thought was heaven on earth, I found myself gagging and spitting! I had just sampled my own feces!

A slap upside my head told me the whole story. "BOY, DON'T YOU EVER SHIT IN YOUR PANTS AGAIN AND LEAVE THEM IN THE BATHROOM FOR ME TO CLEAN UP!"

"Look, I made some homemade peanut-butter just for you"

DEVIL IN THE WINDOW

One night when I was four, my momma was in the kitchen cooking dinner while I was in my room playing with my toy soldiers. I think it was Halloween. The house we were living in was between Sylacauga and Sycamore, Alabama on a little hill. So, we were basically living by ourselves out there. I decided to go see momma because the aromas from the kitchen were calling me. I walked down the hall. The hall emptied into a large living room with a big picture window. Upon turning into the living room the picture window was straight in front of me, and there was the Devil!!! His face was looking right at me! It scared me so bad that I screamed! I ran into the kitchen and grabbed onto momma. She asked, "Butchie, Butchie what's wrong?" I said, "There is a devil looking at me through the living room window." She of course walked into the living room to look and hollered back at me, "Larry, honey there is nobody out there." "Come in here." I replied, "No." "Come on sweetheart, there's nothing to be scared about." I walked into the living room and, sure enough, there was no face in the window. Was it my imagination? Was it really the Devil? Or was it Halloween and some fool had a devil's mask on just looking in the window messing with me? I'll never know, but I know one thing: it scared this little man to death. I almost peed in my britches. But, relating back to the Peanut Butter Story, I damn sure don't want to drink my own piss!

ICE TRAY

I remember when I was five years old. I would take turns spending a week or two with the grandparents, either on my mother or father's side. One particular summer I was staying a couple of weeks with my grandparents on my mother's side, the Johnson's. I remember being in the kitchen with my grandmother Florita; I called her grandmother. The other I called maw-maw. I always addressed my mother's parents as grandmother and grandfather. I remember standing in the kitchen with my grandmother and her pulling out an ice tray to make a cold drink. Well, back then the ice trays were made out of metal and there was a handle that you pull up on and it would break the ice cubes apart. She set the ice tray on the table. I was five years old and it was hot. I thought to myself, "I think I'll lick this." I picked up the ice tray and as soon as my tongue hit the bottom of it, I was stuck! I'm mumbling, "Muumuu hum sum shellpp me." My grandmother turned around and said, "Oh no Butchie, your tongue is stuck!" "Hold on, let me get some water and I'll get it loose for you." While she was at the sink getting some water so that my tongue would come loose, I panicked. I went ahead and ripped it off; by doing so, the top skin of my tongue came off with it. Needless to say, that was some extreme pain for a child of five to endure. My tongue bled for a good day and I never stuck my tongue to a frozen, metal object again!

MY FIRST FISH

When I was five years old, I found myself with my mom, dad, aunt and uncle up on a river just outside Sylacauga, Alabama. My uncle had a little fishing cabin up there. Mom, dad, and myself had gone up there for a weekend to visit and do a little fishing on the river. I remember my dad and uncle sitting on the dock fishing. I was just walking along the water's edge catching frogs and bugs.

At one point, my dad said, "Larry, come here and hold this pole for a few minutes. I've got to go up to the house; see if you can catch a fish." I said, "Yes sir." I walked up on the dock and sat down next to my uncle. While I was holding on to the pole my uncle said, "Larry, you got a fish! Reel it up." I started reeling; my heart started pitter-pattering at ninety miles an hour! You want to talk about exciting; I had never caught a fish. I was scared and excited at the same time. What a unique feeling! I managed to get the fish up to the top of the water; he was fighting and flopping and splashing. I'm sure my uncle helped me pick it up and get it on the dock. I do remember it turned out to be about a four-pound fresh-water catfish, which is damn good eating. I forgot all about it for years. But then as I got older and was teaching my children to fish it came back to me. Sometimes they would get bored, I'd hook into a fish, hand them the pole and say, "Oh look, you've got one." And they would bring it in and thought they had caught the fish. So I wonder now, is that what happened to me? Was there a fish already on the end of that pole and they let me reel it in thinking I had caught it? Or, had I really caught a fish on my own? I guess I'll never know the true answer, but I do remember my first fish!

HARD TIMES

The slamming of the door brought me awake that night. Loud voices, yelling at each other.

"Where have you been?" she demanded. "Only out drinking with my friends," came the reply. "You're drunk again, you bastard!" she yelled. "Oh yeah? You bitch, take this!" as his fist struck my mother like a car wreck crashing.

Leaping out of the bed, I had had enough of this abuse to my mom, I was ready to defend her. At six years of age it didn't matter.

I jumped him from behind, he shook me off like a flea. "And this little bastard has pissed me off as well!", he screamed. Picking me up by the neck, he threw open the backdoor to our small house and tossed me into the backyard.

"Ohh Strick, don't do this to our only child", she begged. "Fuck the little som'bitch", he said, as the door slammed shut on my life.

At six years of age this could be a traumatic thing, thank God I had been through this before in a previous lifetime.

Now I am on my own, now the wind chills my bones. It's nineteen degrees out in the yard, and I'm freezing. No one to help me. What do I do? Only one thing... survive!

You know it is an amazing thing how God watches over the little children. I looked around and saw pine straw and leaves. Lying down, I covered myself with what God had

11

provided. Warmth and some comfort lulled me off to a fitful sleep.

That morning, I awoke to the sound of my father leaving for work. I knocked on the door, and my bruised mother answered. "Oh God, Larry are you alright?" "Only a little chilly", I said through chattering teeth. "Come in and I'll make you a nice warm breakfast. You'll have to forgive your father, he was drunk." And I thought to myself, what does drunk mean?

Later, as I went through the last of my days at six years of age, I laid in my bed and vowed unto God. Never, in my life, will a child (if I ever have any) go through what I went through.

And as the tears roll down my face as I write this, to my mother and father, all is forgiven.

BAPTISM BY FIRE

Ah, the sweet dreams of a six-year old. All wrapped up and snuggled up in my bed, content and happy, until suddenly the slamming of my bedroom door awakened me. In walks my drunken father, singing some bar room limerick and flopped down on the bed next to me. My mother would not let him sleep with her because he had been out drinking all night.

He lay there and mumbled, groaned, and sang. I silently (after a few minutes of being scared out of my wits) slipped out of the bed and walked around it, but I had to walk by his side to get out of the door. I was going to get in bed with momma. So I tiptoed, as cautious as a hunter sneaking up on his prey, trying to get out of the bedroom without awaking him. I was almost there; another three feet and I'd be free. Approaching the door, he suddenly sat up and leaned over to puke on the floor. Instead of hitting the floor, he hit me from head to toe in vomit! And so at an early age I was baptized by fire.

THE FIRST ACTING ROLE

$\mathbf{I}$ was in the first grade and we put on a little skit. I don't know if you folks remember the old story about the three Billy goats gruff and the troll that lived under the bridge? The Billy goats tried to cross over the bridge to get fat, first the small one, then the medium sized one, last the large one.

When I was at the age of six, I was very big. I wasn't fat, very thin actually, but big. The teacher picked me out of the tryouts to be the troll. I was the mean, ugly troll that lived under the bridge. I remember they took a pillow and tied it around my stomach and put an old shirt on me to look bigger than I was. Of course I was a little squatnot anyway, so I imagine I looked pretty funny. Little short legs and a big belly, I probably looked like a troll! They put makeup on me, glued a fake beard on, and put on a hooked nose. I was one mean looking troll.

They had built a little bridge that I was to hide under. I remember the first little Billy goat came walking and I jumped out, did my routine, and then got back under the bridge. The second Billy goat came to cross the bridge and I jumped out, scared him, and back under the bridge I went. Now remember, when the third Billy goat came to cross the bridge he jumped on the troll and killed him, then they all walked over to the other side to get fat. The third Billy goat (the largest) came to cross the bridge and I remember jumping out. After two or three times getting out from under the bridge, my pillow was getting loose. I jumped out and went to do my little acting job to scare him, well when he jumped off the bridge to attack me, the pillow slipped out and fell down to the ground at my feet. And of course I could hear the parents laughing because they thought it was cute. Well I didn't think it was cute, I was upset. Now what am I going to do? I had looked like the mean old, fat troll. Now I'm not fat anymore and here's my padding lying on the floor next to me. I remember hearing them laughing and I looked down at the pillow, and at the audience. I just stayed in my spot because, as the story goes, I was dead, defeated by the biggest Billy goat gruff. That was my first acting role.

THE BEGINNING OF MUSIC

It started when I was a very young child. I had a fever. I found myself surrounded by vibrations of musical notes. The feeling it gave me was one I could not ignore.

First grade, they gave me two sticks to click together and make music. I was hooked, everyone else had bells and tambourines.

Second grade, my mother bought a compilation of classical music. It consisted of several albums of the masters like: Brahams, Beethoven, Chopin, etc. I used to put the records on our hi-fi and pretend I was the conductor leading the orchestra. One day when I was eight years old I conveyed to my mother, that I would like to play piano. And so it began.

Mom bought me an upright piano and I started taking piano lessons. It started off very simple. Chopsticks and then the basics, all the notes. The first year was easy. The second year was a little bit harder (I'm nine now). The third year became a little more difficult. The fourth year started to challenge me (I'm eleven). I'm into playing classical music now, sight reading the compositions (for those of you who don't know what sight reading means, it is looking at a sheet of paper with musical notes on it and transforming them from paper, to mind, to fingers on the keyboards). It's tough. In the meantime, I have self taught myself guitar. Some older guys (thirteen to fifteen years of age) that I knew could play twelve-string guitar, four-string tenor, and wash tub bass. (A wash tub bass is a number three washtub turned upside down with a sawed off broom handle about four feet long with a notch that fits on the rim. It has a piece of twine or rope tied at the top connected to the center of the bottom of the washtub; the rope is plucked with the hand and creates a bass tone.) The guys and myself (playing a six-string guitar) formed a band.

At that time, Folk music was happening; Kingston Trio, Peter Paul and Mary, etc. were hot. Now remember, I am only eleven years old! About once or maybe twice a month we would get a booking to play a job. We would make about twenty dollars a piece (this is 1961). Back then at eleven years old that was damn good money. Better than bagging groceries or delivering newspapers. As a result, the classical piano became a burden onto my young mind. Instead of taking the hard road, I took the easy way. "MONEY!" And then after a year and a half of playing Folk music the BEATLES arrived. Now I'm hooked.

One day there is a talent contest at school, so I get up with my guitar and play three or four songs that I had written, granted I don't remember what they sounded like now. If you put a gun to my head, I couldn't tell you what they were or what the words were. Ha-ha! So I do my tunes, I get off stage, I didn't win but it didn't matter. I got up there and got to play. Two chicks that are in a top-forty band approach me, and they go "We've got all the instruments, we don't need a guitar player but you sing real well and we need a male singer." And I'm going, "Okay." I've been playing for money and fun so let's go in a full band, electric. Ooh, get scary, electric! Yeah, now we're talking, electric. So we rehearse and we start playing gigs at the navy bases, community centers, private parties and what not.

The band lasted a year or two, and then I moved on to another band, doing Beatles, whatever was out there on the top forty. (Beatles, Zombies, Dave Clark Five.) So I did that for a few years. I graduated from high school. By now the Doors have come out, Acid Rock is starting to hit the scene now. The hippie movement is starting to blossom. And I'm talking flower power baby. Well along come the drugs. Now we're playing rock n' roll, eating acid, and smoking pot. The hair started to grow. We're rockin' baby! I did this from eighteen to twenty-one (and there are a lot of stories there).

Anyway, when I hit twenty-one I realized that I'm not that good of a singer, compared to all the ones that are out there making it. So I figure well, I'll stay in the business 'cause I love playing music, it's good, the women are fine, and they're free. I figured there's plenty of bass players and guitar players, but not that many keyboard players. I had piano lessons when I was a kid, so I'll get me a keyboard and start learning how to play again. And so it began!

Within four or five years I'm starting to play keyboards pretty good, plus I'm singing. Making money, making a living (sometimes). Every once in a while we have to resort to eating a pack of peanut butter crackers and a Coca-Cola for the whole day. But we're free. Isn't anybody looking over my shoulder telling me what to do. I'm proud. Playing rock n' roll, I'm a music man! Damn right. So about the time I was twenty-four or twenty-five, I had learned how to play pretty good. I kept playing, started traveling a lot. Over the years I've played everything from Top Forty to Acid Rock, Blues, Southern Rock, Reggae, and Country and Western. I have just about covered all the bases as far as an entertainer goes. But from my younger days, the classical training, I learned to have an understanding for the finer forms of music like jazz and classical. And so my quest still continues. And I figure that I will keep on playing until the day I die. And so I put it this way. My job in life is to make you, as the listener, forget your daily struggles, the stress and the strife that you go through. The good Lord blessed me and as a result I am able to make your time on Earth a little bit better.

THE FIRST DRINK

Now I'm about seven or eight years old. My momma and daddy had a problem with drinking. It had its good and bad moments. I remember my first drink that went along with my first oyster. One Friday night my dad and mom and the couple who lived next door to us were having a little get together under the porch.

They were going to shuck some oysters, fry up some shrimp, and just have a general party to blow off some steam. They'd been working all week in the factory. I was standing out there and I remember my dad and his friend Leon shucking oysters and drinking whiskey out the bottle. They were looking down at me and asking, "Larry, have you ever had an oyster?" I said, "No." "Well, try one," they said. So I said, "Okay." They shucked one and put it on a cracker for me. They said, "Now take this cracker and let the oyster slid into your mouth. Then as your chewing it up take a bite of cracker and swallow." I tried it, and damned if it wasn't good! I stood there like a little bird with my mouth open, waiting for them to shuck another one and give it to me.

After my dad had gotten a buzz on he said, "Well Leon, I think this boy is turning into a young man and I think it's time for him to have a drink of whiskey. He's never had a drink of whiskey, what do you say?" Leon answered, "I don't see why not, he's your son Strick." Daddy said, "Larry, do you want a sip of whiskey?" I said, "Yes sir." He said, "It's gonna burn a little bit." I asked, "You mean like heat, do I have to blow on it?" He said, "No it's just the taste of it. It's kind of hot and warm. So take you a little sip." He handed me the bottle and helped hold it for me. I remember tilting the bottle back and taking my first sip of whiskey. When that shit hit this young man's mouth and throat I thought I was going to puke. But I managed to swallow it down. They were looking at me and laughing while tears were running down my cheeks. I just stood there looking at them and I asked my daddy, "Can I have another one of those?" And I've been drinking whiskey ever since.

He handed me the bottle and helped hold it for me.

EAT A PEACH

When I was nine years old, my mother and father had separated. So, to get away from my father, my mother moved my sister, my brother, and myself to a house in the country that belonged to my mother's girlfriend's parents who were farmers. They were harvesting peanuts at the time, I never knew that peanuts grew out of the ground. When you're nine years old, peanuts come from a jar or a bag!

I had fun up there. The family had a big barn. There was a garden hose hooked up to a gallon bucket with holes punched into it, which was the outside shower. They had pigs, chickens, and a few heads of cattle. It was a big family. I think there was something like seven or eight kids. There was a little boy about my age, nine or ten years old, and we became buddies for the couple of weeks I stayed there.

I remember getting up one morning; his mother made these huge breakfasts consisting of scrambled eggs, fried eggs, biscuits, sausage, ham, bacon, and grits. She'd spread it all out on this big, long table that would sit about fifteen people, unbelievable. After waking up to the smell of breakfast cooking, my buddy and I were sitting on the porch watching the sun come up. There were some peach trees in a field about twenty to thirty feet away from us. My little buddy asked, "Larry, ever had a fresh peach off the tree?" I said, "No." He said, "Come on." So, we walked over to the tree and I remember reaching up and picking a peach right off the tree with the morning dew still on it. I remember putting the peach in my mouth and taking a bite. The juices just exploded out of it, all over my chin and my cheeks. I looked at my buddy and said, "I've never tasted anything that good!" He said, "It's wonderful." I went to get another one and he said, "No. Momma will get mad if we get filled up on peaches and don't eat our breakfast." So I said, "Okay." About that time we heard his mother calling all the kids in, and his daddy and older brothers out of the fields; time to eat breakfast. They had gotten up at four thirty and were already working. One thing I'll always remember is the taste of my first peach.

RUNNING TO PRACTICE

At age thirteen and in junior high school, my father wanted me to play football. I had no desire to play football. I didn't want to get hurt; I don't like pain. But, I played because my father wanted me to. I was actually forced to play football.

One day, while in the eighth grade and about fourteen years old, school got out and it was raining. I thought, "I am not going to practice, it's raining." I wasn't about to play in the rain, so I got on the school bus and went home. We lived about five miles from the school. I got home and was there about thirty minutes when my father came home from working in the factory. He looked at me and said, "What are you doing here?" I said, "Well, it was raining. I didn't go to practice." He said, "Did you ask the coach if you didn't have to practice?" I said, "No sir." So he got on the phone. A few minutes later he said, "Come on. They're having practice. You are going to practice." I went to get in the car and my father asked, "What do you think you are doing?" I said, "I'm going to practice." He said, "No. You are running to practice." My father made me run from our house to the school and he followed me in the car. Like I said, it was about five miles from our house to the school. When I got there I was completely out of breath, completely exhausted. I was young though, and I could handle it. My father got out of the car and went up to the coach and said, "Here you go coach. He thought he'd get out of practice because of the rain." The coach looked at my dad and said, "You made him run all the way?" My dad said, "Damn right." The coach said, "Go get suited up Larry." I went and got suited up; my dad had left by then. The coach said, "Larry, go over there and kneel down on one knee. You don't have practice today." Thank god for the coach because I was so tired from running five miles I wouldn't have been worth a flop anyway. I never was that good at football; my heart wasn't in it. I played for two years and that was the end of my football career.

FIRST TIME STONED

I was sixteen years old and just starting high school, when I had to get a physical for PE class. Part of the physical was having blood drawn. I'd never had blood drawn. Sitting down, the nurse stuck a needle in me and pulled out a nice size syringe full of blood. She put a piece of cotton on my arm, a Band-Aid, and said, "You're done." I got up and walked out of the lab room. My mother was a few doors down by the elevator. Approaching her, she punched the button on the elevator, turned, looked at me, and asked, "Are you alright?" I said, "Yes ma'am." And that was the last I remember until waking up in a hospital bed.

I had passed out and fallen straight back on the tile floor and my mother couldn't catch me in time. I hit my head pretty hard and was out for about three hours. Well when I woke up in the hospital later that afternoon, my mom and dad were there. They asked how I was feeling and I asked, "What happened." They told me and I replied, "My head and neck hurt and my arms are tingling." It was like my arms were asleep from my shoulders to the tips of my fingers. You know that tingling, prickly sensation you get when your foot or hand falls asleep? That's how my arms felt. This went on for about two weeks. Evidentially I had pinched some nerves in my neck. After a couple of days of complaining about the prickly sensation, the doctor prescribed some medicine for me, which was supposed to be taken once a day in the morning. I had forgotten by the third day and accidentally taken it twice. About two hours later, I was sitting in a classroom and I looked around and had the strangest feeling of being there, but not there. Realizing that I was stoned on narcotics, morphine to be exact, I started itching. So, the next day when I got up instead of eating one pill I ate two and liked it. Needless to say, the following two weeks went by in a haze. But, I sure was happy!

FIRST SURFING EXPERIENCE

I was sixteen years old and a freshman in high school. I had an older buddy named Jimmy that I went to church and school with. My buddy had a car and would give me rides so I wouldn't have to ride the school bus; my momma and daddy wouldn't let me have a car.

One day we were out riding around and Jimmy said, "Let's go surfing." I said, "I don't know how to surf." He says, "I'll teach you." So I agreed. We got our shorts, put the surfboard through the back window, and down the road we went. We headed down Pensacola Beach (before it was developed). We pulled off, got out and the surf had two and a half to three foot waves, not bad for Pensacola.

Jimmy got on his surfboard and paddled out. He got up on his board, bent over on his hands and knees, caught a wave and stood up. He must have ridden it a good twenty or thirty feet. I was standing in waist deep water thinking that it didn't look that hard. Yelling for him to do it again, he did it two or three more times as I watched. He couldn't tell me how to do it because I couldn't hear him over the waves crashing.

Finally, he asked me if I was ready. "Yeah!" So I got out on the board, paddled out with my legs hanging over the side, watching the waves. Spotting one and deciding it was good I started paddling just before the wave got to me. It picked me up, and I was gone! I got on my hands and knees and tried to stand up, but I lost my balance! I stepped forward and the front end went straight down. I flipped and went under with the waves crashing down on me. Well, the board also went straight down but then it shot straight up in the air about ten feet. I stood up and the board came down

31

and knocked me out! Face down in the water I went. Jimmy was about fifteen feet from me; he swam over and flipped my face out of the water. If it wasn't for him, I would've drowned. What I had done was 'pearled' the board. That was my first and last surfing experience.

CANNED HEAT

At age eighteen, I was working for my grandmother and grandfather on my mother's side. They had a small combination Tastee-Freeze and restaurant where they made hamburgers, chicken boxes, etc. My grandfather was starting to go blind from diabetes, so every once and a while I'd take him to the store or to pay a bill. My grandparents had helped me buy a 1957 Chrysler; it had an eight-track player that I installed. Grandfather always played a harmonica pretty good. In fact, he showed me how to play. I started playing blues harp for a while. I had gotten a new Canned Heat album (a late 1960's psychedelic blues band). The band consisted of Bear, a big guy who was the lead singer, Blind Owl, who played the flute, guitar, and sang. Their biggest hit was "Going Up the Country".

One day, we were driving down the road and I put the Canned Heat album in. My grandfather went absolutely nuts over this band! He loved it! He asked me who they were and I explained everything to him that I knew about them. So it got to the point where we'd be sitting around, grandmother would be cooking and I'd be sweeping or mopping. Then I would hear grandfather say, "Butchie, lets go for a ride!" Whenever he said that, he wanted to get in the car and just drive around listening to Canned Heat. God rest his soul; he passed on several years ago. I'll never forget my grandfather Johnson's love for the blues harmonica and his love for Canned Heat!

FIRST TIME BUSTED

Around early 1968, a bunch of my friends and I were partying in Fort Walton. There was about two or three guys that were sharing an old house with lots of party rooms. About a dozen of us had gotten hold of some really good LSD. I mean this stuff was pure electric dynamite! So we all dropped at the same time. Everyone was having a good time partying.

About three or four hours later, we all started to peak; it was very intense. The next thing I knew, none of us could move. We were all so stoned that we were just laying on the floor, propped up in chairs, and draped across the back of the couches. No one could move except one little squirrelly fellow that was always hyper, his nickname was "Crab." He had started tripping right along with the rest of us and was peaking. All of a sudden, he looked around and realized nobody was moving! He flipped out and thought everybody was dead! So out the door he ran and down the street he went. We lived about a mile from the cop shop. He ran all the way to the police station and screamed, "All my friends have died! They're all dead!" The cops are asking, "What?" He replied, "Yes, all of them, they're all dead." So they put him in a cruiser and drove him back to the house. They walked in and here all of us are stoned out of our minds and moving our heads a little bit asking, "What's going on?"

The cops brought a bunch of cruisers, piled us all in, and took us back to the station. They knew we were doped up. Then they started questioning all of us. Well, luckily no one had any pot on him or her, or any illegal drugs; we were just stoned to the max on LSD. So after about two hours tripping in jail cells, asking each other, "What the fuck's going on?" They came out and said we could all go home. We all just looked at each other wondering why, because here we were tripping in jail on LSD. They kept asking what we were on and we told them, "LSD." They said, "Well, y'all can go home because LSD is not illegal."

This, like all the rest, is a true story. I was doing LSD back before it was illegal in the United States of America.

"All my friends have died! They're all dead!"

THE PILL BOTTLE

It's 1968, a friend of mine, Ed Rankin, and myself, were cruisin' around town. He had a fifty-six Chrysler, old beat-up hunk of junk, but it was a cool car to cruise in. I think gas was about thirty cents a gallon, smokes were twenty-five cents a pack. Anyway, we had some marijuana in a prescription pill bottle. Every once in a while, we'd pull some out and twist up a joint to smoke. Then lay the pill bottle back on the seat between us.

So we were riding around, it was about eleven o'clock p.m. I'm eighteen years old. Ed turns to me and said, "If we get pulled over, there is a hole over the transmission hump in between us on the floorboard. Drop the pill bottle down that hole and we won't get busted." Sure enough, here come the red and blue lights. The cops have got us. As we pulled over, I dropped the bottle down the hole. After I let go of it, the bottle fit in the hole but the top didn't! So the cap of the pill bottle was visible. It looked just like a cap top lying on the floor.

The officer asked us to get out of the car, patted us down, and asked us what we were doing out that late in that part of town. We told him we were just cruising around. He was suspicious of us because of our hippie looks. He searched the car, but never touched the pill bottle top. He told us to get in the car and to never come back in his patrol section late at night. So, we got back in the car and spilt. After our hearts stopped racing and we had calmed down, Ed said, "Boy that was close. Thank goodness for the hole in the floorboard. All we lost was some pot instead of going to jail." I looked at him and said, "Ed, look at this." And pointed to the top lying on the floor. He said, "What is that?" And I bent over, grabbed the top, and pulled the bottle up that had the pot in it. We both started laughing so hard we cried. Only one thing to do, roll a doobie, and smoke another.

THE BANANA STORY

It's 1968; I was playing in a group called the Shaydes. Playing at a semi-hippie club called the Electric Experience named after Jimi Hendrix's first album. I was just a lead singer back then. We did a lot of LSD and we were playing basically the stuff that was out in '68 (Hendrix, Cream, Doors, etc.).

One night we were tripping on acid, playing at the club, which was complete with two go-go dancers on each side of the stage in cages with bars wearing white go-go boots. They were fourteen and fifteen year old girls just a shaking as we played our rock 'n roll.

There was a grocery store next to the club. I was pretty much stoned out of my mind and I decided that I'd walk next door and buy a banana. I came back with the banana and it was time for us to play our first set. The club was set up with a big, giant stage, about ten rows of folding chairs and behind that was an area where people could dance or stand around. Since I was the lead singer, the band started playing and I came walking out with a banana stuck down my pants. Looked like I had a damn nine or ten inch hard on. Teenage girls were going nuts! Pointing, laughing, and jumping up and down, squealing and hollering. We had played about thirty or forty minutes and we were really getting into our music. We were sweating. We were really putting on a big show. Well right in the middle of a good number, I was grinding and hunching and bumpin', 'cause I'm a young rocker. (Not looking to bad in those days). I reached down my britches and pulled out this big banana. I took it and threw it out into the audience. To my surprise, about a dozen girls fought over catching that banana. Peeling and eating it.

41

The next night, we were getting ready to do the gig and all the little girls were coming up asking, "Are you gonna do the banana thing again?" I asked, "Why?" "Because we love that. We fought over the banana last night and we want to do it again." "Okay," I said. So during the whole summer of '68 I had to put a banana in my pants and about half way through the first set throw it out to the crowd. And the girls would fight over who got to peel it and eat it. And thus, the banana story was born.

SNORT BOMBS

$\mathbf{I}$n my earlier days of smoking pot I never wasted any. My friends and I would even take the seeds and stems and boil them down to make tea. Whenever we finished a joint, we would either eat it or snort it. Nothing was ever thrown away; we used all the parts. Sometimes we would hold the roach in between two paper match heads and fire it up. We'd let it burn for a few seconds, blow it out, and snort it.

One day while my brothers and I were sitting around smoking roaches, I came up with a great idea. "Instead of rolling a joint", I said, "Let's try something different." I took a rolling paper, put a bud in it, and wrapped it up real good. I put two kitchen matches on each side of this little ball I had made and wrapped it in paper. It was about the size of a fifty-cent piece. Then I commenced to setting it on fire; I let it burn for a few seconds, then blew it out. After the ceremony was finished I snorted it. Well, needless to say, it was pretty rough on your nose, lungs, and eyes. You've heard the old song, "When Smoke Gets In Your Eyes." It would damn sure do that.

My friends and I would snort these along with smoking our joints. It was just another way to get high. But, it was always fun just to sit around half drunk, stoned, and decide, "Hey man, let's make a snort bomb." And away we would go, snorting our way to heavenly bliss.

FROG LEGS

Late 1968, my bass player friend Richard, and myself were living in a two bedroom cottage on Highway 98 just outside of Ft. Walton Beach, Florida. We were playing in a four-piece rock band, The Shaydes. We didn't have a lot of gigs because we were an acid rock band.

We were usually starving our asses off from lack of money. We would go out and pick up coke bottles on the side of the road. After cashing them in, we'd have just enough money to buy one Kentucky Fried Chicken dinner (one serving meal). Sharing the dinner between the two of us, we would suck the bones dry. The next day, I would boil up the bones and make chicken bone soup! Times were pretty tough.

In downtown Fort Walton, there was a little seafood restaurant with a chest freezer out back. The only thing on top of it was a cement block; the owners didn't lock it up. One night, about midnight, Richard and I were pretty hungry. We took his pick-up truck and drove behind the restaurant. Everything was all closed up and locked down. We were really taking a chance 'cause there was cop patrols everywhere. We threw the cement block off, opened up the freezer, and found boxes and boxes of frog legs from India and likewise of French fries! We grabbed about four boxes of frog legs and the same amount of fries (each box was about twenty-five pounds). We loaded up his pick-up truck and off we went.

Problem was we did not have a chest freezer; all we had was a refrigerator. So, we took the door off the freezer compartment, turned the controls wide open, and made it into a giant freezer. We stacked all the frog legs and French fries inside. For three weeks Richard and I, and whoever else came over, fried up frog legs and fries. We weren't hungry for almost a month! By the end of a month of eating frog legs everyday though, I came to the conclusion that I never wanted to eat another frog leg again! And I never have!

THE DEAD WAGON

In late 1968, the band I was playing in had a buddy, named Ted, that helped book our gigs. He was a drug dealer and helped us cop drugs. He also had a van to tote equipment in, so he was an all around friend. We used to listen to a lot of blues back in those days, along with all the acid rock groups that were out. One old blues song in particular, was about "looking out the window and seeing the dead wagon roll by, taking another soul to the graveyard."

One day Ted picked me up and said, "Come on we're taking a ride. I got something to show you." So I said, "Okay." We got in the old van, cruised down the road and pulled up in someone's yard. There was a black hearse sitting outside, a late fifties model. Ted said, "This thing is for sale." I asked, "How much? And does it run?" "Yup," he answered. "They only want fifteen dollars." We paid the money, got the title and off we went.

We had so much fun with those wheels. We immediately named it "The Dead Wagon", after that line from the blues song. We would take turns getting stoned, lying down on a platform in the back with the curtains drawn back so people could see us, and pretend we were dead on our way to the graveyard. Who wanted to be dead next? That was the joke. Picture us riding down the road, longhaired hippies driving and pot smoke pouring out of the windows. It was good for a few laughs.

We also used "The Dead Wagon" to haul musical equipment to our gigs. When we would pull up to the club, everybody would flip out. Almost all the girls would want to go for a ride and get stoned in "The Dead Wagon". And, we would oblige them every chance we got! Needless to say, the back of "The Dead Wagon" was not only used for toting our gear.

INTENDENCIA STREET

In the winter of '68, a couple of musicians, myself, (and the guy who booked the band and bought the drugs), rented a house in downtown Pensacola on Intendencia Street. There was always parties going on, of course. One night in particular, we were sitting around playing a board game that was invented by Ted, the guy who did the bookings. It was called "The Muff-Muff Game." After you rolled the dice, you moved your joint (game piece). We had different colored joints: strawberry, banana, chocolate, and white. You moved it so many squares depending on the roll of the dice and whatever square you landed on you had to do what it said. For example, draw from the pile, and in the middle of the game board there was a pile of cards to draw from. One of the cards might have said, "Shotgun the person directly to your left two joints." Or another card might say, "You must get shotgunned by two joints." For those of you who don't know, a shotgun is when someone holds a lit end of a joint in their mouth and blows smoke into a second person's nose or mouth.

A couple of girl friends of ours stopped by. They were going to Junior College in Pensacola. One was from Fort Walton, the other from Syracuse, New York. We all played the "Muff-Muff Game," and we went through one or two lids (about two ounces). After the game, we all retired to a room to watch TV, a little while later the girl from Syracuse passed out on the bed. We all laughed about it. Thirty minutes later one of the guys said, "Man, I think something is wrong with this chick." So, we all started checking her out. Sure enough, her face was white, her hair was plastered to her face and she was not breathing! We started to resuscitate her with CPR. Well, she would not respond and we called for an ambulance. Before they came, we cleaned up as much pot and paraphernalia as we could. The E.M.T.s arrived and said, "She's dead," and away they went. Then the cops showed up. They took us down to the police station and asked questions; they hassled and harassed us. There was nothing that they could do until the autopsy.

Six months went by. Nobody was arrested. We didn't hear anything. The roommate (from Fort Walton) of the girl, got called down to the station about every six months and got questioned by guys in plain clothes. This went on for about two years. Finally, her mother and father went down with her on one occasion. They demanded to know what was going on with their daughter. Come to find out, the girl had a medical problem with the blood vessels in her brain (I don't know if it was an aneurysm, tumor, etc.). She was not supposed to do any kind of speed whatsoever, whether it was caffeine or any type of stimulants. She had taken some acid earlier that day that had Strychnine in it (which makes you go fast). As a result she died on us that night. The reason it had been kept quiet so long was because she had been a member of a group to over throw the government up in New York. The FBI thought we were a southern splinter group of this organization. So the FBI told the police not to arrest us and for two years they followed us around! I was one of the guys that the FBI followed around, for two years, and didn't even know it! Once they found out that we were not a revolutionary southern group trying to over throw the government, but a bunch of drugged out rock 'n roll musicians, the incident was quietly forgotten. But, I imagine somewhere deep in the bowels of a basement warehouse storage room you can find my name in the FBI's almost wanted list!

MUSHROOMS AND PEANUT BUTTER

All righty then... now I would like all you readers to sit back and take a real deep breath... let it out slowly... alright one more time... deep in... ease out... feel better?... you should...you have just injected thousands of microscopic, teenie-weenie, itsy-bitsy, spores... spores that the good lord lets float around in the air... sometimes floating down just after a nice rain shower... falling down and landing on a pile of cow shit... suddenly between the spore contact and the cow shit a certain wonderful chemical reaction transforms... a mushroom is born... a nice, smooth, all natural, organic, hallucinogenic... guaranteed to give you a nice, little, nonscary high... you will trip and laugh... in fact, you will turn into a moon face... the first time I came into contact with actually harvesting my own mushrooms... it was just after a rain... it had rained on a Tuesday evening... Wednesday morning my buddy got up and said, "I know where there's a pasture with cow shit in it and maybe there might be some mushrooms. Lets go hunting."... so we did... we drove down some country roads outside of Pensacola... found this cow pasture off a little dirt road and it was at the bottom of a hill so unless you stood at the top of it you couldn't see what was going on in that part of the pasture... so the farmer couldn't catch us... we climbed over the fence... sure enough, we picked a bag full of the sweetest little mushrooms... bless their hearts, they're so pretty... let me describe... imagine a beautiful mushroom about six or seven inches tall, with about a three to five inch diameter hood, light beige in color, dark purple underneath, and on the very top... looking down upon it... the good lord took an airbrush gun and made a perfect yellow circle there that in the middle, about the size of a dime or quarter, depending on the hood size, it just kind of sunbursts there... it's beautiful... well anyway... we got us a bag of these things and off we went... we were safe... I asked my buddy,

"How we gonna eat these?"... he said, "Just take a bite of them."... so we took a bite and we started gagging... good God... so we pulled into a convience store, went inside, and got a loaf of bread and a jar of peanut butter... came back out and made mushroom and peanut butter sandwiches... we ate one apiece... by the time we drove from north Pensacola to downtown Pensacola where we were living... we were some giggling, stoned out, freaks... hmmm... I'd like a mushroom now please...

We made mushroom and peanut butter sandwiches.

THE NIGHT I DIED

My buddy and I had been shooting heroin for about a year. Late one night we were finishing up a gig at a club in Pensacola when he said, "Let's go get some heroin down on the blocks," (which was the local place to cop the drug). You would drive along slowly until you made a connection with a dealer for a balloon of heroin; a small balloon was fifteen dollars. I said, "Okay. Let me borrow my girlfriend's car." She was a good old gal and I borrowed fifteen dollars and the keys to her car.

My brother man and I went off on the mission. We got in the car and he said, "This is what we're gonna do...we're gonna rip them off. You drive, scrunch down in the seat and drive real slow, and when I find a connection they're gonna walk over and you stop. I'll get them to hand the heroin in; I'll still be holding the money. When I say, 'Looks good', you punch it and get the hell outta there!" I said, "Okay." Next thing you know, we're cruising the blocks and he tells me to stop; we've got a deal. We stopped; the man walked up, handed the dope to my buddy, and he said, "Looks pretty good." So I punch it and we burned rubber outta there.

We headed back to the club to pick up my girlfriend and go to her apartment. She was not into the heroin thing. But she was willing to put up with it though 'cause I was a rock 'n roll musician. My buddy said, "We're gonna split this balloon up. You get the first hit." I replied, "Okay." He split it up in half, cooked it, loaded up the needle, injected it into my vein, and the rush came. I was feelin' wonderful. The next thing I know I was in another room coming to. I said, "Whoa, I got off on that shit." They said, "Yeah you did. You died asshole!" I asked, "What do you mean?" They came back with, "You fired up that half a gram of China White,

55

your eyes rolled back, and you had no pulse. You were dead!"
Thank God my brother reacted in time. He mixed up some
salt water and found the old needle opening and injected it
into my system. Then he started pounding on my chest, got
my heart pumping again, and revived me.

The next day they told me the whole story of what
had happened. I thought to myself, 'Damn, I'm only twenty
years old. I want to be a rock 'n roll star, too young to die
now.' That was the last night I ever did heroin. Of course,
it took me two or three months to get over the Jones and
give it up, but I've never done heroin since because that was
the night... **I DIED!**

Larry Strickland

THE RED DEVIL TORNADO STORY

$\mathbf{I}$ was playing in a honky-tonk on Pensacola Beach called the Pier Lounge. Two or three of the groups from Pensacola met up at the club on the beach, and we decided it was a jam thing. Everybody took turns getting up on stage, singing and jammin'. Next thing we know, somebody came up passing out the LSD! Course, I don't refuse, let's trip, and let's rock. A couple hours later, I was starting to get off, things are starting to go wiggily-woggily or woggily-wiggily or wibbily-wobbily. I walked outside on a break to smoke a doobie and make the shit kick in a little bit better. I looked up, and there was a storm coming in over our heads. I thought, "Wow, it's stormy." Yeah, whatever, rock on.

At the end of the gig, a friend of mine said, "Let's go to your house and party." I said, "Sure man." I lived about ten miles down the road at a place called Oriole Beach. A friend and myself we're renting a two-bedroom bungalow. As I was riding home, I looked over at my buddy who was driving us and I started to come on heavy. I was starting to peak. He was like a skull with two arms driving. I said, "Oh shit, this stuff is strong." We got to the crib; three, or four other guys pulled up, musicians from the club. We were drunk, stoned, and tripping our asses off!   After we got in the crib, it started storming, and raining, with the wind howling, and trees bent over. We got a little funky stereo, and played the new album from Savoy Brown, titled "Outside Lookin' In." The album had a little dwarf looking into an eye of a skull. It was a pretty spooky album and we were tripping out really hard.

A bass player friend of mine, Sonny Blackwell (big dude) hell of a damn monster bass player has been through tornadoes before. He suddenly said, "Shut up everybody.

57

Shut up and listen!" We all got real quiet quick and we heared something like a freight train bearing down on us. It was a damn roaring sound surrounding us. "Shit! It's a fucking tornado!" he screamed. "Open up the doors, open up the windows, if not this house will blow apart! I've been through one, I know what's going on." So we all immediately jumped up, 'cause we figure he knows what the fucks happening. We opened up the windows, we opened up the doors, and we could still hear this roaring sound. Everybody ran into the back bedroom and I said, "Hell, I gotta pee!" So I walked out of the front door, and onto a screen porch. Telephone lines and electricity lines that surrounded the house were glowing a blue light. And I was thinking, "Whoa. This is heavy, but I still got to pee." Unzip, pull it out. I was not going out of the front porch; I was just going to piss through the screen. As soon as my piss hit the screen, a spark zapped me and hit me in my damn dick! I yelled, "Ouch! That's it. I'm going into the bedroom with the rest of the guys."

I hollered, "Where you guys at?" "Back here in the bedroom," came the reply. I went back into the bedroom, we all huddled up, about four or five of us. Sonny said, "Man, there's a tornado coming, let's pull that mattress up over our heads." My back and my head were up against the wall. All hell was breaking loose! All kinds of sounds from hell are around us. The storm, the rain, the lightning, the roaring, the wind, the thundering. My head was leaning up against the wall, and there was water trickling down the outside of the wall. All of a sudden, it felt like the back of my head had opened up and my brains were melting through the back of my head down the wall! I saw myself on a table, with aliens bending over me. They were looking at me and then they reached over with some kind of instrument and touched me in the chest. About the time they touched me, I screamed, because a fucking cat had come in from out doors and jumped on my chest! You talk about a shock, you talk about a heart attack! If I weren't a strong boy (at nineteen years old) I would have died from shock of that touch as high as I was. I screamed bloody murder and everybody asked, "What's the matter?" I yelled, "The aliens have touched me!" And they said, "No. It was a cat." I said, "Oh, son of a bitch. The cat jumped on my chest. Okay."

Here we were still huddled up, and the storm was still roaring. The door was open to the bedroom. One of my buddy's said, "Look, there's a little red devil standing in the doorway. Look he's about six inches tall!" We all looked and sure enough, there was a little six inch red devil! He was looking at us, and he turned around and ran off. We all yelled, "Whoa, what was that?" About that time, the wind picked up more intense and started breaking limbs and tree trunks; shit was hitting the top of the roof and we were freaking out! Back under the mattress we went. We grabbed hands and actually started saying the Lord's Prayer. "Our Father, who art in heaven, hollowed be thy name, thy kingdom come, thy will be done, etc." We were scared shitless. We were holding each other's hands and hugging like a bunch of kids; been scared for an hour, tripping our asses off, flipping out. The storm finally began to subside.

We all came out from under the mattress, looking and touching each other and asking, "Are we still here? Yeah, we're still here." Okay. Well, about thirty minutes later the sun rose. We walked out and saw the damage from the tornado. There were broken limbs down; it looked like God's war zone. We ended up walking out behind the house (which is a wooded area) and I said, "Man that was one heavy, heavy trip. I don't think I want to go through that again." My friend answered, "Yeah man, that was scary. How about that little red devil?" And I say back to him, "Oh God. Where did that thing come from? Did you see him too?" "Yeah, I saw him. He was about six or seven inches tall." "Yeah, he was. He came in there and looked at us, turned around and ran off." I asked, "We actually saw the same thing?" He replied, "We all saw the same thing." We walked around checking things out. All of a sudden I stopped and looked down at my feet and there on the ground was a unique object. I reached down and picked up a plastic, little red devil. I held it up for the guys to see. They all came over, looked at the devil, looked at each other, and everyone was speechless. We just shook our heads and walked away.

THE PASS

In 1969, the band I was in at the time was moving from Valpariso, Florida to Wing, Alabama. We had moved everything except our crop of young, sweet things (I'm sure you know what I'm talkin' about).

On our way up a particularly long stretch of highway, we encountered a road-gang truck heading back to their compound.

We were smokin' the herb without a care in the world, when we pulled up behind them. The prisoners were watching us toke down and laughing. We were lovin' it, exchanging peace signs and generally fuckin' with them.

We couldn't pass 'cause we of course were in a hippie get-up-and-go van (which means not-get-up-and-go).

They were giving us signals that they wanted some, so I pulled some bud and leaves off one of our sweet, young things and put it in a paper bag.

Finally, we got on a downhill grade. As we passed the truck I leaned out the window and passed one of the prisoners a bag of truly, wonderful smoke. We were all screamin' and laughin' at the exchange as we continued onward.

Lookin' at the driver as we passed, we realized it was a county cop! We punched the gas as hard as we could. Finally, we got far enough ahead to breath a sigh of relief. Needless to say, it was a close call, but I like to think we made those guys' day. I wonder if any of them ever think back to the moment of THE PASS!

I passed one of the prisoners a bag of truly wonderful smoke.

ALMOST FAMOUS

In 1969, the guys and I were playing in a psychedelic club in Panama City. We consisted of bass, drums, lead guitar; I was the harmonica player and lead singer.

One night we got approached by some people that said they were promoters for the first Southern Pop Festival to be held. They went on to say that they would like our band to show up in case one of the acts could not make it, and handed us tickets to get in free. We, of course loved it.

So we traveled to Atlanta. They said just to bring our axes (guitars). Everything else would be provided. Now, I was nineteen years old and a rocker. I was ready to kick some ass!

We walked in for free to this major Pop Festival. It was packed! A band was setting up getting ready for the first act, when suddenly the giant P.A. system announced, "Would the band from Ft. Walton Beach, Florida please report to the back stage!" We jumped up and went backstage. Backstage were our friends that had talked to us and had provided the tickets. They said the opening act had been in a wreck and couldn't make it! "What do you need to start off the show?" "One set of drums, one bass amp, one guitar amp, two mikes and two stands," I answered. "Done," they replied.

Backstage (while their soundmen were setting up our group) we were smokin' the herb, drinkin', and just generally getting fucked up to open the show for one hundred thousand people!

We were ready. Now, finally we can spread our sounds (some original, some re-makes, like The Zombies, and

Steppenwolf). Suddenly someone came up and said, "The band made it!"

So we backed down and the other group got on stage. Being the first opening act, the people loved them! They ended their one-hour set and came off stage. I thought these guys were just like us, a little original and a little re-make on the old stuff.

Immediately record producers approached them. Two months later their album came out: "On Time" by Grand Funk Railroad.

SHIT- ALMOST FAMOUS!

GOING TO CALIFORNIA

August 27, 1969; it was Saturday night. I was turning nineteen years old. The band I was playing in is working at the Odyssey Club in Panama City; rock n' roll hell, heaven, which ever way you want to look at it, but we lived in Fort Walton. The cops had already warned us if they even caught us stopping at a store to get gas or cigarettes they were going to throw us in jail, cut off our hair, shave us bald, and make us work a couple of days on the road gang. I saw some guys come through there that had long hair. We met them and about two days later they saw us and said, "Remember us?" (bald headed). I said, "No." One said, "I'm Tony. The cops got me because I was walking down the street with long hair." They shaved his head and made him work on the road gang. So, as a result, we would travel back and forth from Ft. Walton to Panama City about fifty miles one way.

We were having a big birthday party at the house that I was renting; a hippie house. Everybody was messed up; we'd been partying all weekend. Well, actually we've been partying for a couple of weeks. So, little did we know there was a narcotics agent, sheriff, cop, wannabe, that worked at the gas station, pumping gas. Okay. So he knew where some hippies lived. He was trying to be Mr. Big Time. Mr. I'm "cool", the hippies suck. So he had been coming over during the week and spying on us. We were high, eating LSD, smoking pot, and drinking whiskey. What the fuck, over? We were making plastic zilches! Do you know what a plastic zilch is? You take a dry cleaning bag and roll it up into a long tube, twist it up, hang it up on the ceiling, put something on the floor to catch the plastic when it melts, then you light the bottom end of it and it starts burning. It makes a sound like: zzzzmmmmppp, zzzzmmmmppp, zzzzmmmmppp. So we were making plastic zilch melt things, which are real cool to look at when you're stoned.

This punk narcotics agent had been peeking through the windows watching us partying. Watching us smoke dope, watching us make plastic zilches. Well, here it was my birthday; there was about fifteen to twenty of us in there. I had put my notice in to quit the band on Saturday night. I had put my PA system and what little clothes I had into my van; I had a giant traveling van, heavy duty shocks, and big tires. I was gonna go to California to be a rock star! I was nineteen years old and ready to go!

While we were all partying, I said, "Okay guys. I'll see y'all later. I am going to get in the van. I'm going to California." I opened the door, swung open the porch screen door, looked up and got punched by a giant fist! Back through the door I went, flat on my back; I looked up and it was a county cop about the size of the damn Hulk! Behind him came about twenty cops, one right after another! Yada yada yada yada yada. They surrounded us. They looked at us and said, "We got a search warrant for doing drugs in here." We said, "Umm, okay." We were locked down; the cops have got us. They search us one at a time. Made us take our boots off, stripped us down, and looked up the crack of our butts (that hurt, by the way). They made us open our mouth, checked our hair, and went through all our clothes. Then they let us put our clothes back on and sit in another room. Blah, blah, blah. I had forgotten about two hits of LSD that I had stashed in a stick of butter, in the refrigerator; they found that.

Sitting there we started messing with them. We were saying, "Hey man, you better take that air conditioner apart, take the damn cover off and check behind the filter. Might be some drugs in there." We were giving these guys hell. We were nineteen years old, to hell with the cops!

Know what I'm saying? I said, "Did you check the heel of my boot? I've got a special heel." A cop ran over and yelled, "Let me see that boot!" He tried to take it apart and I said, "Screwin' with you man." I didn't give a shit. I was pissed off 'cause I was on my way to California! Soon as I got in my van I was driving to Los Angeles, San Francisco, whatever came first. My ass was gone!

One of them came up and asked, "Who owns the white van parked across the street?" I said, "Me." "We want to search it. You can either let us search it now or we can get a search warrant for it." I said, "Okay, well I ain't got nothing in there, here's the keys, search the motherfucker!" So they got the dope dog. Let me tell you, on the way back from the club that night we'd been smoking opium. You have to put tin foil in a pipe, make a hole, put the opium inside, and when you smoke it the opium swells up. It blossoms like a flower. We'd smoke a couple of hits, I'd take the tin foil off, wad it up, throw it over my head and it'd land in the back of the van. Load up another piece of tin foil, poke a hole, fill it up, smoke it, wad it up, and throw it over my head. Reload. I had like seven or eight little balls of opium wadded up in tin foil in the back of my van. The dog got in and they came back and said, "You're under arrest." I asked, "For what?" "Five marijuana seeds in your glove box." And I said, "Is that all?"

Down to the jailhouse I went, I am not going to California now! They impounded my van because it had five marijuana seeds in the glove box. I said, "It was bird seed, for my bird. I was toting birdseed." Back then, they used to actually put marijuana seeds in birdseed; it was a mixture of sunflower seed, etc. They impound my van; I went to jail for a week in Crestview, Florida, which is the county seat for Okaloosa County.

After a week locked up, I got out, got my van out of

the impound, and my dad was mad as hell at me. He said, "I helped you get that van, I co-signed for that van. You take that van and go down and clean it up 'cause I'm selling it. You drug addict!" "Yes sir," I replied.

I went to clean the van out and what did I find? About seven or eight pieces of tin foil, balled up with opium in them. The drug dog, supposedly, sniffed five marijuana seeds in my glove box, but couldn't find opium balled up in tin foil in the back of my van? Come on. What kind of drug dog was that? Anyway, I never made it to California.

Larry Strickland

THE SMOKING HELMET

Back in the early days of my ganja smoking, my friends and I would come up with different ways to get high. One example is to take an ounce or "lid" and roll it up in a newspaper to make a giant, foot-long joint.

One night we were sitting around and came up with a new way to get high. We took a large, brown paper bag, cut a rectangle out in the front, covered the hole with Saran Wrap, and sealed it up so that when the person's head was in the bag you could see their face. Next, a person would take the bag, put it on, and roll it up around their neck. They would have to hold it shut. Then, they would sit there while we cut a hole in the top.

Next, we'd fire up two fat doobies and shotgun the smoke into the hole until the person's face was no longer visible through the front. Once that was accomplished, we would pinch off the hole that we were shotgunning through, and the person would sit there and slowly breathe in the smoke until the bag was clear. By the time they had breathed in all the marijuana smoke and the face shield had started to clear up, it was so funny to be on the outside looking in! Watching someone's face as they finally inhaled all the smoke. Their eyes would be red and glazed, and they'd have this stupid grin on their face. Once they breathed in as much smoke as possible and the face shield was finally clear, we would remove the bag. Smoke would be coming off of their hair. Kind of like a Cheech and Chong thing, it was a funny way to get stoned.

Every now and again we'd sit around and decide to make a smoking helmet. Away we would go with our paper bag, scissors, Saran Wrap, and doobies, to turn one person's world into 'smoking helmet heaven'.

71

A person would take the bag, put it on, and roll it up around their neck.

THE PROCOL HARUM STORY

We were playing in a club called the Intersection, across from the old Jax's Brewery Company in New Orleans, Louisiana. We were a Rock n' Roll Band. The club was really hip; this was where all the really good bands played. We went over there about once every two months; it was basically just a weekend gig between the club and a few others. We were there about two or three weeks, partying, and raising hell; and I'm talking raising hell in New Orleans in 1969! We were "giging" there one weekend and the group Procol Harum, "Whiter Shade of Pale", etc. was playing a concert in New Orleans. Well about midnight, we were playing a set and a couple of long hairs walked in. You could tell by the way they were dressed that they were rock stars, they were not just your average hippies; they had a certain persona about them.

When we finished our set, we got off stage, and one of the guys came up to the guitar player and myself and we started talking. Back then I was still just a lead vocalist, harmonica player, and tambourinist. He introduced himself and said he was the lead guitar player for Procol Harum. I said, "Wow, cool man." He gave our guitar player a compliment and said, "You sound just like Eric Clapton," which was a great compliment at the time. We ended up going out to the van, smoking some herb, snorting some coke, drinking whiskey, drinking beer, and just generally getting fucked up.

So we went back into the club and we were still on our break; we sat down at a table together. The lead guitar player of Procol Harum, myself, and the guitar player (that I work with) sat there talking and bull shitting. I looked over at him and said, "Well man tell me, what is it like to be a rock star?" He kind of chuckled. He looked back at me and with his British accent said, "I don't have to ride the greyhound busses anymore." I looked at him and said, "Hell man, I ain't even made it to the greyhound busses yet!" And I never did!

THE SPITTING STORY

In 1970 the band I was in, "The Wing Brother's Band", lived in Wing, Alabama. We would travel to play in New Orleans, Panama City, and Fort Walton. Well, there was a Battle of the Bands in Fort Walton at one point and we were one of the bands that were going to battle it out, to see who was "the best band in Fort Walton."

We traveled down there, ready to play our rock 'n roll. The guitar player, the drummer, bass player, and I were all drinking moonshine and smoking pot. We were getting moonshine at eight dollars a gallon up in Wing, Alabama, which is a damn good price. When we got to the club, we set up our gear on stage one. There were two stages facing each other, while we were setting up, the other band was playing. Everyone was down at their end, listening to them, cheering and dancing.

It came time for us to play; everyone came down to our end to listen. Well, by that time we were pretty fucked up. We had been smoking and drinking the 'shine. We were pretty wasted. We got on stage, kicked off the set, and started rockin'. The people start dancing; they were having a great time. We were kicking ass! Back then, I was just the lead vocalist. During the first song, the guitar player and I were looking at each other singing and we looked at the crowd and decided we were gonna spit on them! So here we were, playing, leaning over and spitting on the audience; instead of getting pissed off at us, they started screaming, "More, more!" They loved it!

"The Wing Brother's Band", stoned out of our minds, drunk on shine, spitting on the audience and they loved it! Of course, I found out years later that it doesn't work anymore.

MEMPHIS

Around 1971, the band I was in sold everything we had, loaded up in a little station wagon with what little music equipment we had, and decided we were going to move to Memphis. Some girls that we knew had moved up there about a year earlier and had a giant house; it was a three-story old Victorian-style home. So we moved, started hanging out, and found us a job. Our first gig started at five in the morning and ended about nine in the morning at a bottle club. The second gig we landed was right across the river in West Memphis, which is actually Arkansas.

We played in a Mexican restaurant, which also had a lounge on the other side. In fact, B. B. King used to work there, when he was on his way up to the top. Staying at the house where the girls lived was pretty cool, but there was one draw back, they were vegetarians. Once a day, around five or six at night, they would cook this giant feast. They had this huge, long table that would seat about twelve people. There would be all kinds of food laid out, but no meat! And I was raised on pig, fowl, fish, and cow.

We chipped in what little money we had for food, but they would still dish out vegetarian meals. Don't get me wrong, the meals were good; they were wonderful, but there was no meat. The girls were taking their supplements. We didn't have any supplements; we couldn't afford any! So after about six weeks, the bass player and myself were driving around town. I looked over at him and said, "I'm so damn weak, I don't have any energy!" He said, "Yeah, me too. It started about a week ago." I said, "I feel like I'm sick, something is not right." Suddenly a little light bulb went off (Bing!); we need to eat meat! We drove down to where we had seen this little Bar-B-Que spot, on the side

79

of a street corner in downtown Memphis. We pulled up and ordered a Bar-B-Que sandwich a piece, and that stuff was so rare it looked like blood was coming out of it. It was so good! We had it all over our faces, dripping down our chins, and running down our necks, staining our shirts. We were in hog (ha ha) heaven. We finished that meal and agreed that it was pretty good; no more strictly vegetarian meals. We would eat them, but we were going to eat meat also! We cannot live without meat; we cannot live without our protein, it's that simple!

Later on that night, when we were sitting around looking at each other, I said, "Man, are you as stoned as I am?" He agreed. (We hadn't had any meat in our system for so long that it was like we had smoked two or three joints or took some valiums; we just couldn't move.) So, for all you vegetarians out there, "Rock on baby!" But, daddy is gonna have his pork and his beef and his chicken and his fish and whatever else I can afford to put in my belly!

PIANO NECK

Have you ever heard the term, "piano fingers?" (For those of you who don't know, "piano fingers" is the term used by musicians for when their fingers cramp up from playing too much.) Well, in 1971 I caught a case of the piano neck! The guitar player I was working with knew a club owner down in Panama City (a cool beach bar right on the Gulf of Mexico). In fact, they did so much business that they would average twenty to twenty-five kegs of beer a night. All they sold was draft beer and there were a lot of drunken kids at that bar.

So, we put together a band to go down and play there for the summer. At the time, Edgar Winter (a national known musician) had started the trend of wearing a keyboard around his neck. I thought that was pretty cool, so I decided to try it also. I took my keyboard, which weighed about thirty-two pounds, got a couple of knobs you use to strap guitar straps on guitars, mounted them to the end of my keyboards, and hooked on two guitar straps so it would hang around my neck.

The first day we rehearsed, I used my new rig, in the garage over at the bass player's house. We stood up for about three hours of solid rehearsal and finally everybody decided to take a break. We went in the house. I sat on the couch while we passed a doobie around. We got stoned, relaxed, and drank ourselves a cold beer. About thirty minutes later, my chin dropped to my chest! I thought to myself, "What's happened?" I could not lift my head up. Everybody looked at me and asked, "Larry, what are you doing?" I answered them with my head down. "I can't lift my head up." My neck muscles had given up from holding the keyboard around my neck for three hours. It actually got to the point where I could not breathe; your head is very heavy. I couldn't lift it up or breathe because my chin was on my chest and I was closing off my esophagus! I could not get any air in my lungs! I had to take both hands and hold up my head so I could breathe. It took about two hours before I was able to keep my head up naturally. And thus, I had a case of "piano neck."

CHITTERLINGS

In 1971, I was playing music with a six-piece group with three African-Americans and three white guys. One of the African-Americans played the congas and various percussion instruments: maracas, tambourines, etc. His name was Smokey. One night, after rehearsal, he invited us over to his momma's house for dinner. When we finished rehearsing, we went over to eat. Smokey's mother was a big jolly woman and she had a huge spread laid out for us. There were vegetables, cornbread, sweet tea, and bowls of mashed potatoes; a great spread. Well, the main course came, was set out in the middle of the table, and everybody started digging in. As I was passing stuff around, Smokey's mother said, "Larry, pass me your plate so I can get you some chitterlings." I said, "What, chitterlings?" She said, "Yeah, you ain't never ate chitterlings?" I said, "No ma'am." She said, "You are gonna love them Larry!" For those of you who don't know, chitterlings are pork intestines that has been stuffed with meat and spices and then cooked. Well, I went ahead and started eating. I tasted the chitterlings and damned if they weren't good! In fact, I went back for seconds, but that was the only time I have had chitterlings prepared by a proper cook. So, I haven't tried them since.

MARRIAGE NUMBER ONE

In 1974 my first child, Gabriel, was born to my first wife and myself. She had helped me get off of heroin, so I thought I was truly in love. The marriage only lasted three years before we got divorced. Through the years I have seen my son grow up, graduate, join the Air Force, and come out. Most recently, in the year 2002, his mother (my first wife) passed away.

Over the years, I have not seen Gabriel that much, because he has been traveling around the country doing his thing as a young man. Now, he has a pretty cool job; he is a light technician. He travels with some of the newer groups fifteen to twenty-five year olds would listen to. I am proud for him; he has become a good young man. He is doing real well in this life.

As far as his momma goes, I did love her, she did help me out. She got me through a time of need and distress. And I hated to hear of her passing. I guess I'll see her on the other side one day.

STEEPLE JACK MAN

In 1975, married with my first son, music wasn't going too well for me. I had just started teaching myself how to play keyboards after being a lead singer for years. My gigs were kind of few and far between. As a result, I had to find another form of income to take care of my wife and child.

I landed a job with a painting company in Pensacola. The only stipulation was, it wasn't houses. I had to go up high, painting office window trimmings and their fire escapes. I said, "Well I can do that." On the first day of my job, we had to paint the Empire Building, which was Pensacola's first tallest building, at eleven floors. I would open up the window and get out with my safety harness. I hooked into the painter's eyehooks that were wielded onto each side of the window so I wouldn't fall backwards. Then I would scrape the old paint off and put a couple of coats of new paint on.

I noticed a giant water tower going up in downtown Pensacola during the painting of the Empire Building and, when that job was done, I went down and talked to the guys at the water tower. They had just started sand blasting the tower, which had taken six or eight months to construct. I met the foreman, a good 'ole guy named Charlie, and he asked me if I had any experience. I pointed to the tallest building in downtown and told him I had just finished painting it. I was kind of familiar with spiders, stages, and bosun' chairs. He said, "Well, okay." Of course, I would smoke a doobie on the way to work every morning.

I hired on with the company. We finished the sand blasting, priming, and then we started putting on the vinyl, rubberized paint. As some of you might not know, tall buildings and structures over a certain height have to be able to bend and sway with the wind. It might be calm down there on the ground, but at a hundred and fifty feet up in the air, the wind is constantly blowing. I had been working there about six months, making really good money, and the tank was the second tank ever built (at one million gallons); the first was in Atlanta, Georgia. As a result, the spiders that we used (driven by hydraulic air) would not go quite high enough because of the new design. To accommodate, they had constructed a six-foot extension rod; you would go up and let your weight down on a chain attached to your spider. (A spider was a waist-high cage that you worked out of.) Then, you would stand up on top of the spider cage and attach your cable onto another hook, then lower yourself down. You would get the chain off, bring your cable back up, then go up another six-feet in the air. The foreman asked me if I knew how to do it and I said, "Yeah." Well I didn't know how to do it. As a result, I was in the middle of trying to get my cable loose when my chain slipped. If I had given it another good jerk, the cable would have been off, the chain would have come loose, and I would have dropped about two hundred feet to the ground. Needless to say, when it happened I only dropped about six feet. I didn't fall out, but it scared the shit out of me. The boss man saw it and told me to come down immediately! It was lunchtime anyhow; he asked me what happened. I told him and he said, "Man, next time you have a question, please ask. Don't try to figure it out on your own." And I never did.

When it came to working up high, if I had any questions at all I always asked the man with experience. Because, that little six-foot fall taught me a valuable lesson. I would not have been able to write this book, lived the life I've lived, if I had jerked that cable a little bit harder!

LOUNGE LIZARD

During the first fifteen years of my rock n' roll career, I thought I was going to be a rock star. My band played the hard, heavy rock. We played our own music and tried to make it big traveling around the southeast. We spread the word of rock n' roll. As the years went by, I realized that it wasn't going to happen. But, I still continued to play music.

As I got older, I had a family, and I had to make a living. You might say I sold my soul to the devil. I started working in lounges with bands playing the top forty cover songs. We were basically just a live jukebox. It sucked in a way, but at least we got a paycheck.

People like me back in those days, the pre-disco days, were called "Lounge Lizards." I am sure you have heard of "Bar Flies", the women who hang out in the bars, but for the musicians who had to bow down and play the top forty in a bar for a paycheck, we were "Lounge Lizards."

THE STRANGEST THING

In 1979, I was playing in a band at a club on Pensacola Beach. It was a fairly decent sized club, but what was unique about it was the stage had a bar shelf around it. So, if a customer sat there you could reach out and touch them on the shoulder. In return, they would be able to sit there and watch you up close, which could be a good thing, to some point, and bad at others.

We had been playing off and on there for about a year. One night, something happened on the dance floor (the dance floor was packed by the way). Suddenly, there was a commotion going on. I was sitting down playing keyboards so I couldn't see what was happening. I stood up and looked and everyone was gathered around one couple. The crowd was hooping and hollering. Finally, it cleared out enough where I could actually see what was going on.

Here we were, playing our rock n' roll music, everybody dancing and having a good time, and in the middle of the floor there was a chick on her knees in front of a guy standing up with his britches down; she was going to town! A rock n' roll blowjob! I have to admit out of all the years playing music there has been a few weird things happen...but that is definitely the coolest and strangest thing I have ever seen while playing.

THE PRINCE OF DARKNESS

In 1978, the group I was playing with had traveled to Orlando, Florida to play a gig. I can't remember exactly where the job was. We got to the hotel we were staying at, unloaded our clothes, and took showers to go play. Suddenly, I hear the sounds of diesel buses pulling into the parking lot. I looked out the window and said, "Holy shit man. There are three silver eagles (for those of you who don't know, a silver eagle is a tour bus favored by entertainers)." I was thinking to myself, I wonder if it is Black Sabbath, because they were doing a concert across town.

So after the gig, we came back around one o'clock in the morning. I remember standing there unlocking the door and seeing this group of musicians; they were staying about two doors down from us. I could tell they were musicians and they could tell we were musicians (we both had the look). We starting talking and yep, it was Black Sabbath. They asked, "Hey guys, what are you doing?" We said, "Well, we just got finished with a gig." "How did it go?" "Pretty good." "Why don't we meet down by the pool and have a few drinks?"

We changed out of our clothes, which were soaking wet (we did a lot of sweating in those days) and went down to the pool. We started trading stories and talking music. Next thing I know, Ozzy sat down next to me! We sat there until dawn drinking whiskey, smoking, laughing and having a great time. And let me tell you something right now, Ozzy has a beautiful, beautiful spirit. I had a great time the night I partied with Ozzy Ozburne, The Prince of Darkness!

MY FIRST RECORD

In 1978 I was playing in a Country and Western band. We sucked! We consisted of two keyboards, bass, drums, pedal steel, guitar, and a chick vocalist. I think I was making like a hundred and fifty dollars a week. Whoopee! In the mean time, I had written about four or five country tunes. A friend of mine, a big drug dealer, respected and liked me. He had heard my tunes and said, "Larry, here's the money. Let's cut a forty-five." I said, "Okay."

I got the guys together and we worked up a couple of my songs. We practiced for a couple of days. After we got it down pretty good, we start playing it at night for the crowds, in a club we were working at. Next thing you know, we started getting requests for it. The title of the tune was "Whiskey's My Companion." By now I was starting to feel pretty good. People were requesting it, they were dancing to it, and we were getting tipped for it! I thought, how cool is this. We went into a local studio here in Pensacola. "A" side is "Whiskey's My Companion"; "B" side is "Funny How Love Can Die." To master it, we had to take the tape to Nashville. My friend (who was backing me up) and myself got in his Jaguar and headed up to Nashville. I think we snorted like a half an ounce of cocaine on the way up. Yee-Haw! When we got there, we took it to a mastering studio, and dropped it off. They said it would be ready in two days. So here we were in Country Music City, my friend and I. We had two days to blow in the city. Look out! We did the tourist thing. We even checked out the Country Music Hall of Fame.

After we got it mastered, we dropped it off at another place to get it pressed, and we pressed five hundred copies! When we got back to Pensacola, they shipped the forty-five's to us. I had customized the label myself; it looked real good. In fact, I've got two of them left; they're mounted in a frame on my wall. The only two left I imagine.

I took a few and passed them out to the local Country and Western radio stations; fortunately, I knew a DJ at one of the stations. I asked him to listen and play it if he wanted. A couple of days later I was sitting at the house, listening to the radio. Suddenly, I hear the DJ announce, "And here's a song by one of our local groups and a good friend of mine, Larry Strickland, singing "Whiskey's My Companion." The song came on and I immediately turned up the radio and tears ran down my face. It was a proud moment for me. To finally be able to hear something you have written from the heart, put together with a group, and broadcasted over the airwaves is unforgettable. I'll never forget the first time I heard myself on the radio!

SECOND MARRIAGE

In 1979, I had the good fortune to meet my second future ex-wife. She was a waitress and myself being a musician, we met at a bar. We started dating and she moved in with me after about a year. We lived together for several years before we got married. Out of that marriage we had two lovely girls: Megan who is in college now, and my youngest daughter Tisha who is in high school. My wife and I worked really hard together to build a home for the girls. I had my taxidermy business on the side, but it was a full time job. I was working six and seven days a week doing taxidermy and five or six nights a week playing music. I was burning the candle at both ends.

After fifteen years of being together, we decided to go our separate ways. It was a mutual breakup. We are still friends and I get to see my children whenever I want. She is doing very well for herself. She has her own bar and a good life. I am proud for her. But, it looks to me after being through two marriages and several dozen girlfriends that I am giving up on the marriage and relationship scene. I'll just stick to being who I am, playing music, having a good time, and making people happy.

COMMODE

When I was married to my second wife (divorced since), we were going through financial hard times. Our first child Megan was three years old.

Day in and day out we would argue about money and bills. I repeatedly said, "Don't worry. I've got everything under control."

One day I was cooking supper and Megan came in and said, "Daddy, I've got to stinky." So I said, "Okay baby, Dad will help." (She was just learning the potty training thing). We headed to the bathroom and she turned to me and said, "Daddy, I can do it myself." I stood there and made sure she was all right. Seeing her get squared away, I returned to the kitchen, leaving the door open so I could watch her.

"Everything alright?" I asked. Her little voice came back and said, "Don't worry I've got everything on commode!"

I learned that day that kids watch and say everything that we as parents do.

MAGIC

When my youngest daughter Tisha was six years old, we were driving down the highway together, going to get some worms for a fishing trip.

She was just a chattering on about all kinds of things when suddenly she exclaimed, "Oh Daddy! I had a dream last night!" "Okay," I said trying to suppress my laughter at her enthusiasm for this dream she so excitedly blurted out to me. "What was it about?" I asked. Her eyes grew big and she said, "I dreamed I could fly, Daddy." Her enthusiasm was contagious. I found myself drawn into her world, for suddenly I remembered having a flying dream when I was her age too.

She went on to say how she was able to fly and she could see all of the houses, and cars, and people below her. "That's wonderful baby," I replied. Then suddenly she turned very somber and said to me, "Do you know how I can do that?" she asked. "No," I said. She looked me straight in the eye and said "Easy. I just used my Imagicnation." She pronounced it: e-magic-nation.

Kids do have a sense about them that we as adults lose somewhere along the road. It's too bad really; we could all benefit from using more of our **IMAGICNATION!**

ROLLING DEATH TRAP

I played in a reggae band for six solid years, traveling around the southeast, making good money. But to travel in a band, you've got to have a vehicle that can tote the equipment plus the group members. I had found an old step van for sale on the side of a road; a small one like the Little Debbie Snack trucks used to be. Remember Little Debbie cookies? You can still get that stuff, mmm good. I think I paid seven hundred dollars for it.

The van only had one seat for the driver. Well, that seat had a spring sticking out of it. So on top of that spring, I had three cushions built up so that you could drive. It had no safety belt and hardly any brakes. Only one of the windshield wipers worked (and that was on a soft rain), the heater would run you out of there during the summer and you couldn't get warm enough during the winter, so we nicknamed it the "Rolling Death Trap." The only major trouble we ever had with that van was the alternator went out one time, we had to replace the battery, and buy tires. Other than that, it ran for about four years, carrying us around the southeast.

It finally got to the point where it was just too dangerous to drive. So I ended up trading that van in, and they gave me thirty-five hundred dollars trade in value for another smaller van. I thought that it was a pretty good deal. I only paid three thousand dollars for a dodge mini-van and I bought it when it was three years old. So I thought I got a pretty good deal on the "Rolling Death Trap."

THE M&M PEANUT

In 1988 I was playing in a reggae band. We had been traveling up and down the Coast during tourist season. We were making a thousand dollars a week a piece; of course, we were working our asses off. I was playing hard-core reggae with three other white guys, believe it or not. The lead singer, a little squat-not, sounded just like Bob Marley.

We worked together a total of six years, playing reggae. During the winter months, when the tourist season died off on the Coast, we would travel to Atlanta, Birmingham, Tuscaloosa, Oxford, and New Orleans. And you know we made a pretty good livin' even then, considering flat tires, brakes going out, engines blowin' up, etc. One night, we were in Atlanta playing, it was the end of the gig, we were staying in something that wasn't really a motel. It was two bedrooms, one bath, and a little kitchenette. Kind of like a bungalow. We stayed in it every time we went to Atlanta, it was cheap. At the end of the night, we stopped at a convenience store and everyone got their little munchies. We got back to the room. We were all sittin' around talking about the night, laughing and joking. We were drunk, high, smoking, and passing the doobie. It was a beautiful thing. Our gig was over for the night.

We were four pieces: bass, drums, keyboards, and guitar. The drummer was sitting across the room from me. He had a bag of M&M Peanuts that he was tossing down. Someone said something and we all started laughing really hard, we could hardly catch our breath. My cheeks were hurting, my ribs were hurting, and I was laughing so hard. I looked up and the drummer had stood up, and he was standing there with his hand on his throat, making weird expressions. The bass player and the guitar player were sitting there laughing at him! I looked up at my brother and realized he was choking to death! He had a candy coated M&M Peanut in his mouth, and laughed so hard that when he inhaled, it got stuck! He was walking towards me with his arms straight out like "The Mummy." Pleading! He couldn't say anything; he was turning blue. I yelled, "Oh my God! I've got to put the Heiniken-Manourvere on him!" (Heimlich Maneuver). I jumped up, ran behind him, put my fists together underneath his rib cage, and jerked him up. He was a skinny little fellow.

I jerked up on him and nothing happened. Well, by that time the bass player and guitar player realized what has happened. Now they were serious. They yelled, "Larry, do it harder!" And I said, "Okay." Wham! I gave him the big ultimate push-shove-lift up and POW! Out popped a candy coated M&M Peanut. He sat down, caught his breath, and we were all concerned now. We were all kneeling around him, touching him, and saying, "Are you okay brother man? Are you alright?" He looked up and he had tears in his eyes because he hadn't been able to breathe. He finally caught his breath and looked over at me. He said, "Larry, you saved my life." He then got up and walked over to where the M&M had flown. He picked it up off the floor, put it back in his mouth, and chomped it down. I replied, "No problem my brother."

Bless his heart. I loved him to death, what a great drummer. Every time we played together, I would turn around and there would always be a smile on his face. He was a beautiful man, great man, and had a great spirit. I hope he's still out there and I hope he gets to read this book. I miss him and his M&M Peanuts!

He was walking towards me like "The Mummy".

SCOTT FREE

In 1991, a blues band group "The Divin' Ducks", which consisted of some Pensacola boys, traveled to St. Thomas in the Virgin Islands to play at a club called Barnacle Bill's. We had a four-week engagement. It was pretty cool living on the island. We got to see iguanas, giant termite mounds, and other things you would not see in the United States. It was beautiful.

I had met this young lady who offered to take me out and show me around the island. So, on my day off we met up at the club where I played. We piled in the car, had a couple drinks, and off on the tour we went. St. Thomas is only about twelve miles long and two to three miles wide. She took me around and pointed out different things to me; one spot was where Fleetwood Mac had their island house. She took me downtown and showed me the movie theater. What's crazy is, when you go inside, if there is a movie playing with a bad guy, all the women and children will scream, "Kill him! Get him Mon. Get him Mon!" The whole theater is screaming back at the screen.

We were cruising around and she pointed out a road. She said, "That is the Scott Free Trail. It's where William Scott, the pirate, got away from either the British or Spanish Navies that were after him. He had sailed into the main harbor and was on shore when he saw his pursuers sail in behind him. He ran to an old goat trail that went up and over the biggest hill on the island; he had another ship anchored in a cove for just such an emergency. (Sounds like Hollywood, doesn't it?) Hence, the term 'He got away Scott Free' was started, pertaining to anyone that escapes a desperate situation."

For you historical buffs, the term 'Scott Free' is an old Scandinavian phrase meaning payment free.

DAVE MASON

Playing at Barnacle Bill's in St. Thomas, I met Dave Mason, the old rock 'n roller from the late sixties, early seventies. One of his biggest hits was "Only You Know and I Know." Also, he later teamed up with Stevie Winwood to form a group called "Traffic." Another one of his hits was "Feelin' All Right."

Dave really took a liking to my keyboard playing. We got to talking and hanging out with one another; he had a home in St. Thomas with a recording studio and he invited me over. I went over about three in the morning; I was pretty trashed. We talked about all kinds of odds and ends. He wanted me to go downstairs and listen to some of his new stuff in his recording studio.

We went to his studio and he had some good, fresh music. He asked me, "How would you like to lay down some keyboard tracks?" I said, "Well, sure Dave." He said, "You know, there is no promise that I will use these tracks, but at least I'll get an idea of how your keyboards sound with my new material." So, I was fortunate enough to stay with Dave Mason for a couple of days and lay down tracks on some of his songs. I don't know if he ever used my keyboards or not. But, it was great pleasure to meet an old rocker I looked up to and I'll never forget that.

SHARK ENCOUNTER

The group that I was playing with, "The Diving Ducks Blues Band", stayed for a month in a nice, little place on the side of a mountain, overlooking a beautiful lagoon with crystal clear waters in St. Thomas. There was a two-man boat with a paddle and we rounded up one pair of fins, a mask and a snorkel. Three of us got out one day, the guitar player, bass player, and I. We took turns getting in the water, holding onto the rope at the front of the boat, paddling around, and pulling the boat behind us; all the while, looking at the beautiful coral and tropical fish. Well, my turn came; I put on the fins, mask, and snorkel and grabbed the rope. I was swimming around for about fifteen minutes and it was just beautiful. I was thinking to myself that all of it was nice, but I'd like to see something a little more exotic. Suddenly, I got a prickly sensation. I stopped swimming and looked up. About thirty feet away from me was a six-foot long blue shark! It was lazily swimming parallel to me; I barley swam, just treaded water while he swam by. I'll never forget he had a parrotfish hanging out of his mouth; for those of you, who don't know, a parrotfish chews on coral. They are a bright turquoise blue. The shark evidently happened to swim by, see this parrotfish, and just chomped down on him! He obviously wasn't hungry or he would have swallowed it and not let it just hang out of his mouth. I hovered there and watched as he finally swam far enough away where I couldn't see him any longer. As soon as he was out of sight, I literally jumped out of the water and told those guys, "Boys, get me in the boat 'cause I just saw a shark!" They helped me get back in the boat and we paddled back to shore. That was my first, and hopefully last, true shark encounter.

About thirty feet away from me was a six-foot long blue shark.

SKUNK AND SNAKE

In January 1996, I was in a three-piece group, "Jezebel's Chilln'." We traveled to the West Coast of Costa Rica to play a two week stint. We arrived there on New Year's Eve. The club was pretty cool; we were playing outside on a very large, covered deck. They had a small gambling room, blackjack, craps, etc., and a restaurant with three course dinners; waiters were dressed in bow ties. It was very ritzy for a third world country and the food was excellent.

The club had put us up in a house about a block from the gig. I was sleeping in the living room; Cathy and Donna were sharing a bedroom. In the living room there was a fireplace with a grate for scraping out the ashes after a fire. Well, the grate was open to the outside. One night after the gig, Cathy and I were sitting on the couch talking. I was smoking a joint and a little animal's head came up through the hole. He was looking around and he finally crawled out of it. It was a skunk!

I told Cathy, "Do not move, whatever you do." We didn't want to get sprayed. He was kind of curious, but he never got out of the fireplace. He just walked around and sniffed a little bit, looking at us. Back in the hole he went, back to the outside. When it was over with, we laughed about it. Then we promptly forgot about it.

Close to the last night we were there, Cathy and I came back from the gig. Donna was in a meeting with the club owner. My glasses were up on the counter in the kitchen. Cathy walked in and said, "Larry, there's a snake in the house!" I said, "What?" "Yeah, there's a snake in the fireplace!" I walked over, I was half lit, looked and said,

"That's not a snake." I didn't have my glasses on, I could see something but it did not look like a snake. I put on my glasses, came back in the living room, and looked. "You're right. It's a snake!" She was flipping out, I was flipping out, and of course the snake is just laying there curled up minding its own business. The club owner and Donna walked in about that time. And I said, "Herbert, there's a snake in the fireplace and I want it out of here!" Herbert walked over, looked and said, "Oh, that's just a baby python." (It was about six-feet long). He took a broom handle and gave him a gentle prod. Slowly, but surely, the python got the message. He stuck his head in the hole and slithered back out into the great unknown. I looked at Herbert and said, "I'm not sleeping in this living room where a snake can come get in bed with me." So we went and got a couple of cement blocks and covered up the hole.

Between the skunk, snake, and vast unknown, I had had enough of Costa Rica.

STUFF THIS

A lot of people have known me for years. They know I have been a musician and grown up in the Pensacola area playing music all my life. But, what a lot of people don't know, is that for about fifteen years I became a respected taxidermist, winning awards at the National Taxidermy Association Competion in 1985.

The first five years was a learning process. To get my techniques down, I used trial by error. After five years, I had perfected my art. I was pretty proficient in freshwater and saltwater fish, also in mammals, such as deer heads, foxes, raccoons, etc.

I rather enjoyed doing this because when I graduated from high school I started going to Junior College here in Pensacola and was going to major in art. I wanted to do some type of artwork as my career. Of course, that didn't work out. I only lasted two years in Junior College until rock n' roll sucked me back in. But, there is an art to doing taxidermy work. For example, when you mount a deer head the expressions have to be just right; you have to know the anatomy of the species you're working on. When it comes to mounting fish, you have to use an airbrush and know how to blend your paints to achieve life-like results so that the customer is happy. Nine times out of ten, my customers were happy and came back to see me. Repeat business, but I was trying to play music at night and do my "stuffing" during the day.

After about ten years, the arthritis in my wrists got so bad I had to take a year off from everything. I had to shut down. I was burning a candle at both ends, trying to make a living, trying to take care of my family, trying to pay the bills. No time for any fun. So now in my old age, I realize it was all well and good when I was younger. But now, I have a laid back and simple life. I try to be as stress free as possible, and enjoy the days on this Earth with family and friends because as you all know, life is short.

STRICK 9

Over the years, I have been called many things. But, my favorite is the nickname I acquired in 1969: Strick 9. In 1968, I tripped for the first time and the acid was from Sweden. It was clinical LSD that they were using in experiments, studying the minds of psychotics and soldiers. It was very clean, pure LSD. As I mentioned in an earlier chapter of this book, I was doing LSD before it was illegal.

LSD came in many types of forms, some more powerful than others. There was "window pain", "micro dot", "paper smears", "strawberry barrels", "purple haze", etc. Some of the LSD that started coming through in '69 had been tampered with and "boosted up". The LSD would be laced with strychnine, which is a highly toxic poison. But, consumed in micro doses into the human body, it has a "speedy" effect.

Some of my friends and I tripped like this for over a year. One day we were all sitting around getting high. One of the guys, knowing my last name was Strickland, yelled, "Strickland, come over here and hit this joint". But, it came out as, "Strick 9, come over here". Everyone started laughing and thought it was really cool because most of the acid we were getting had strychnine in it. So from that day forward and even into the present day, I am still called Strick 9. The nickname has a special place in my heart.

FLORA-BAMA STORY

Connie Tampary and Joe Gilchrist had driven through Alabama to a point, which is now Orange Beach. As they stood looking across the Alabama point inlet, Connie pointed to a stretch of beach sand that distended away to the east. "My family owns several miles of that," he said. Joe was not impressed because there was no access to the expansion of land. Several years later the Tampary's, armed with their vision of the future, tried to get Alabama and Florida to build half a bridge each that would connect. Florida refused, so the state ceded their state line, which was at the pass and moved it back about a mile. Alabama built the entire bridge themselves. Alabama's state line became how it is today by Florida giving up that line.

The road and bridge was completed in 1962. Florida eventually built a road up to the state line, where the Flora-Bama was originally built. After the roads were connected, the first bar on Perdido Key was an old river boat called "The River Queen." It was a honky-tonk facility with a red-clay parking lot. Drinking, gambling, prostitution, and drug-smuggling were rampant in those days. It was basically frontier land back then.

The Tampary's started building the Flora-Bama Lounge, but just before it opened, it burnt down. The rumor is that the "people of the River Queen" burnt it down due to competition. The Tampary's rebuilt and opened in the summer of 1964. Because of the fire, they hired a night watchman, Mr. Frank Brown. Back then the Flora-Bama was in the "middle of nowhere." It was so far out that when it rained the phones would be down for a couple of days because of cheap wiring. There was hardly any police protection, so Mr. Brown came in handy. He worked there six days a week from midnight to eight the next morning when the club opened. Mr. Brown always kept a rifle with a couple of six-shooters on the premises. His presence kept the business from robbery along with other things.

Joe Gilchrist took over the Flora-Bama on April 17, 1978, his birthday. Mr. Frank, as Joe affectionately refers to him, was a very wise and knowledgeable man. He worked at the Flora-Bama until he was ninety-one years old.

The original Songwriter's Festival was a function that Joe and some of the other musicians put together to honor Mr. Frank. They invited him and his lady out one Sunday and entertained them. Ken Lambert was the first entertainer to work at the Flora-Bama, starting in 1978. Joe would be up in the front package store when folks would come in to purchase a bottle or beer. He would invite them in and buy them a drink so they would listen to the entertainment. Within a few weeks, the business had picked up. Ken worked there for about one year and then Jay Hawkins came on board; a little bit later, Jimmy Louis hitchhiked over from Fort Walton and joined the team. In 1979, hurricane Fredrick threatened to blow away the Flora-Bama. But, the bar persevered and opened within a week following the storm after being flooded with sand and mud. The Flora-Bama has gradually added additions from one year to the next. It has become more involved in community activities and charitable events, both to Alabama and Florida.

As Joe thinks back on Mr. Frank, he remembers some of the stories, "mule boy" for example. A mule boy was a fellow who would take the mule to the mine and load him up with ore. One day, Joe asked Mr. Frank what exactly a mule boy was. Mr. Frank said, "Well, if the mule ain't standing where he's supposed to be, I picks him up and puts him there." Mr. Frank was a very big man with extra large hands. Also, in his lifetime, he was a prize fighter in 1917 and then became a professional gambler. At one point in his gambling stint, he would buy a case of cards, open them, mark them, and then seal them back up. He would go out to the little saw mill circuits and sell them to the stores cheaper, about half of what they usually paid. After this, he would go back to the towns to gamble and the people would be playing with his marked cards. When someone accused him of cheating, he would say, "I'll give you five dollars to go buy ten new packs and I'll beat you just as bad as I did with these", knowing they would be buying his cards. Mr. Frank was an amazing character with insight into people and Joe learned a lot from him. He worked at the 'Bama until he was ninety-one and passed away at ninety-three.

In 1984, Pat McClellan joined the team as Joe's partner. Within the United States, the most popular "sport" at functions was throwing cow patties. In 1985, Joe, Pat, and Jimmy Louis decided to create a function in a slow section of the year, April. It was going to be named "The World's Greatest Beach Party". Among a list of things to do at the Flora-Bama's party, Jimmy Louis had the idea of throwing mullet; thus the "Interstate Mullet Toss" began. Joe thought it was just bizarre enough to attract attention, so they included it in the theme. The first turnout wasn't great because of the weather. But, over the years, it has turned into a huge event. There has even been a video made about it, The Mullet Men.

One of the special events that the 'Bama presents every year is a take-off of the "Woodstock" festival called "Sandstock," because we are on the beach. Several of the musicians from the Flora-Bama, from different groups, get together and form one large group called the "Old Hippie Band." We all dress up in wigs, tie-dye t-shirts, and beads to play the old acid rock songs from the late '60's early '70's. This takes place in August. It is a fun event for me because I grew up playing those songs.

I first came to the 'Bama in 1987 with a band I was in. We played the Deck Bar. Over the next couple of years, I came and played with another band I was in. Around 1991, that group broke up and I started jamming at the Flora-Bama with Donna Slater and Cathy Pace. I played with Ken Lambert, Jay Hawkins, Le Ann Creswell, and several other musicians that were working. At the end of the summer of '91, I was hired to work with two groups: Donna and Cathy and Le Ann. I worked with both groups for two years and then split up with Le Ann and just worked with Donna and Cathy; it was too much pressure working with two different units.

What I love about the Flora-Bama is its uniqueness and diverse personalities. You might have a doctor sitting next to a biker, sitting next to a redneck, sitting next to someone who's unemployed, sitting next to a beach bum, sitting next to playboy bunny, sitting next to a CEO of a major company. It is a complete mix of characters, which is a beautiful thing. Everyone comes to the 'Bama to have a good time and to listen to the music.

Joe owns a piece of land across the street from the Flora-Bama called "Boyz Towne." Over the years, he has let musicians and way-word souls live there in their RV's and campers. There have been many bon-fires and parties into the mornings. I have been down there very inebriated many times watching the sunrise. Boyz Towne holds a special place in my heart.

I have many memories from my days on the Flora-Bama team. One memory is from Mardi gras. During Mardi gras, there is a boat parade. All the boats are dressed with a pirate, Mardi gras theme and they dock on Old River. At the time, I was staying in a motor home down by Old River. I had played late into the night before and had no idea of the parade. The next thing I knew, I was shaken awake.

My RV was rocking and I thought, "What in the hell is going on?" I opened up the door and there was about two hundred people packed around my motor home hooping and hollering, cheering and laughing, drinking and raising hell! They were all yelling, "Come on let's party!" I turned around, shut and locked the door, sat down, put my head in my hands and thought, "What a way to wake up."

I'll never forget one night, while I was playing with Le Ann. She thought the bass player and myself were drunk. We weren't. The bartenders had emptied a bottle of Jack Daniel's and filled it with water and coke so the color looked just like whiskey. We were passing it back and forth, pouring it down our faces. The crowd was right there dancing and we would hand it to them and let them know it was fake. They would act like they were grimacing while they drank out of it. Le Ann got so mad at us. When we finally told her it wasn't real, she just laughed. It was a fun little joke.

Once, while I was playing in the main room on a slow afternoon, a customer came in with a miniature poodle; a cute, little dog with a bow in his hair. I was on the microphone calling him and saying, "Here boy, come here boy." And he was running back and forth from each of the two speakers trying to figure out who was calling him! Everybody had a good laugh at that. I sat down at a table during intermission and was waiting for the time to go by. I looked down and realized that the little dog had come up to my feet. Well, he cocked up his leg and pissed on my boot! Everybody got a better laugh on that one; they all said, "He's getting you back Strick 9."

In September of 1998, Hurricane Georges came through. That Saturday night, I had gotten pretty drunk. The next day I was sitting in my RV down in Boyz Towne. The trailer was shaking and everybody on the Key was evacuating, but I was too hung over to leave. I didn't have anywhere to go and I figured I would just ride the storm out. A knock came to the door and it was Jay Hawkins in ankle-deep water asking, "What the hell are you doing?" I said, "I'm watching TV." "Not for long your not, throw some stuff in a bag, you are going with me to Randy (Robertson) and my self's crib." So I said okay, grabbed some items, and we headed inland. I ended up staying with Jay for about three days because Georges was a strong and terrible storm. In fact, the night of the hurricane we were sitting in the living room. Randy went to the front door just to look out at the trees blowing and the wind ripping. When he opened the door and stuck his head out, within a second all I saw were his feet flying out! Because of the pressure, he actually got sucked out of the trailer and landed about seven feet away by a tree! He flew through the air like Superman! I jumped up and called out, "Brother, you all right?" He pulled himself up, brushed himself off and said, "Yeah, but I don't want to do that again." When we finally got back on the island to check out my RV, I was surprised. I half expected it to be flipped over or gone, but it was still standing. There was, however, about three feet of water up to the front door and it took another three days for the water to go down and for me to get power. The Flora-Bama also got flooded, about ten inches of water, sand, and muck; just like back in 1979, the 'Bama persevered.

In 1997, I took a year off from playing because of a combination between arthritis and tendonitis. I had been doing my taxidermy and music playing seven days a week and was burnt out. I basically did nothing but fish. But, I came back in 1998 and Jack Robertson had joined up with Donna and Cathy. Jack and I became pretty good friends and still are today. As a matter of fact, the first year after I came back, Jack and I decided it was the "best breast fest of '98." I had more women take their tops off than I had experienced in my entire lifetime.

In 1999, I took on another job at the Flora-Bama as the sound technician which I still do to the present day. I help set up all the groups that come in and do the sound checks. I also take care of all the music equipment and electronic gear that we have. I have worked the Songwriter's Festival as the "wire dog" and most recently, I have started mixing the sound in the main room for all the groups throughout the two week festival. Welcome Wednesday is always fun. Every Wednesday from the first of January to the end of February the snowbirds come in. The 'Bama provides a main course and our winter guests bring in "pot-luck" dishes. I run the sound for the raffle that follows every meal. Of course, I have been through a couple of pairs of boots during my stint at the Flora-Bama. There is actually a pair stapled (along side all the bras) on the ceiling above where I play my keyboards. What's funny is, about once a year we have to clear out all the bras because there is just too many of them! Then we'll start all over again.

There is one night, around a Fat Tuesday during Mardi gras, I will never forget. I was hanging out in the club and someone said that John Goodman, the actor, was there. I walked up, shook his hand, and talked to him for a little while. I went and bought him a Flora-Bama t-shirt and said, "Welcome to the Flora-Bama." He just grabbed me up, hugged me, and said, "Thanks brother!"

Out of all the clubs that I have worked at in all different parts of the world, the Flora-Bama is definitely the greatest club that I have ever been involved in. And I believe, God willing, I will continue to work there until the day I pass or the day I retire, whichever comes first.

He flew through the air like superman.

POEMS

AND

LYRICS

BAYLEN STREET

It was an unseasonably warm spring of 1968, as I was stoned and walking up Baylen Street.

Old hippies like us were scattered around and found myself in Pensacola's downtown.

Walking along and alone, stoned out of my mind, suddenly looking to my right there was a three story beautiful, old house.

With a for-rent sign on it and the door unlocked, I walked in and said, "Oh my God. What have I found?"

It's perfect for us musicians, us hippies that played around town.

One story, the bottom was not too much to behold, the second story was great, four bedrooms and a bath.

And above that was an attic in which we would trip many times. And up top there a roof, which we could sit on and look as the traffic passed below us.

I called up the realtor and a woman answered, "Yes?" "Is this place for rent like the sign says?" She said, "Yes."

"How much?" And she says, "Fifty dollars a month." And I replied, "I'll be there in a flash."

Calling up my brothers we got together the cash and down I ran to the real estate office and paid her fifty dollars just like she said.

And for months we stayed there and partied we did. We painted the walls and we painted our crib.

We tripped and we laughed and we drank and cried. And we played our music until one of us died.

The old house now does not stand anymore; instead there's a modern day grocery store.

BEGIN TO BEGIN

There's more to love than making memories.
Looking at the mirror through the keyhole,
the artist was walking in as I was walking out.
They are nothing. They are all around us.
I fell in love, and so did the colored man
sweeping the sidewalk.
Do you want to know how to make a lot of
money?
Snow White and the Seven Dwarfs, and how
about a Hi-Ho?
Crackers and chicken salad, slowly killing the
dog.
I haven't been this high since 1947.
If I had only knew.
Ouch, ouch, oh God!
Needless to say, I've still got a finger in my
splinter.
The Mafia does own the A&P.
Jack the one-armed bandit pulled my leg that
night.
Bubbles when it burns.
Singe his eyebrows, that is some real live shit!
Now that is a completed page, it depends on the
do-ers.
TAPES OF WHAT???
Sergeant Fury and his howling commandos.
Yes!
And the butta buttas.

Collect a bunch of local idiots and put them in
the same room together.
And some chocolate covered cheese, topped with
some Bermuda grass.
I'm eating toiletries.
BOTULISM! BOTULISM! HERE I COME!
Get away from you filthy beast, there's a leaf on
my sock.
I'm so tired of fraying; I've got to go to fray at
7:30
in the morning.
I don't know whether to die now or later.
I'm going down to the nearest bar,
To see how long,
To see how far.

THE FLAG FELL IN ATMORE

**(The following poem was written while
traveling from Pensacola, Florida
to Dayton, Ohio).**

The flag fell in Atmore and I was there.
Cruising through town at the designated speed.
We don't want no hassle, from the local
sandcastle. We're carrying weed!
It's a sleepy town, even when folks are walking
around. Waitin' on the train, with the long name,
to reach California so we can move on our way.
I see the sign, Dayton Tires. A place we will
soon be this time tomorrow night.
And behind the sign, a garage spits out the
machine gun sounds of a pneumatic wrench.
In an average front yard sits a tall pine, cradling
gourds eagerly awaiting the purple martins.
At it's feet sit the remains of a huge tree. Its
insides reveal the signs of the chainsaw teeth
that scared the martins away.
Some folks aren't so lucky, abandoned gas pumps
(like azalea bushes) sit in their front yards.
We make it downtown and pass by the
courthouse, they are all so proud of course.
It's Washington's birth, and for what it's worth,
the flags sit like frozen soldiers in a row, hastily
stuck in the walk, in parking meter holes.
As I watch with a frown, one flag falls to the
ground, and a chubby old lady with bookkeeping

hair clip-clops out of the courthouse, a look of patriotic concern on her face.

She picks up the sacred sheet and brushes the Stars and Bars.

What did they say in school? Wash it or burn it? I can't remember.

The flag fell in Atmore, and I was there.

THOUGHTS

I invited my friends
To a revolution.
And nobody came.
Only one or two were ready
For the game.
I've got Montgomery
Tied up in chains.
Roanoke, Virginia says yes
We're the same.

Imagine if the world was run by artists
Instead of fools.
To hell with politicians
And government rules.
If creators of imagicnation
Were in control.
There would be peace inside
Of all our souls.

MEAN OLE' WOMAN BLUES

Jump in the water
Swim in the sea
Just to get my baby
Back home to me
Climb all the mountains
Drive in the cars
Smoke my last cigarette
And drink up the bars

Mean ole' woman blues

Come on home late at night
Found my baby and you holdin' tight
Ain't gonna beat ya or do you no wrong
Just gonna sit down and sing my song

Mean ole' woman blues

Lord if I had a dollar
For every minute I've spent
Try'in to find out
What our love meant
I'd be the richest man alive
And have you baby
Right here by my side

Mean ole' woman blues

WHISKEY'S MY COMPANION

As I looked up and saw her standing there
The room was hot and smoke filled the air
She saw me look and sorta' smiled my way
But I just tipped my glass as if to say

Whiskey's my companion
The bottle's my life
Ever since my children
Went away with my wife
And I'm trying to drown
The heartache and the care
And make believe she really isn't there

Now seasons change
And with it love is gone
The memories of you still linger on
So I'll just turn my head the other way
And dream about our love of yesterday

Whiskey's my companion
The bottle's my life
Ever since my children
Went away with my wife
And I'm trying to drown
The heartache and the care
And make believe she really isn't there

MOVIN' ON

I'm walkin' down the street
My heart's fellin' heavy
Got you on my mind, my knees feel like jelly
Jump back in my car, it's a '49 Sedan
Gonna hit the road, you can have your other man

I'm movin' on
Movin' on
You got me so down
Gonna leave this town
I'm a movin' on - Movin' on

Singing the blues cryin' the tears
You and me baby it's so damn clear
You don't want me and I can understand
Go on with you baby you can leave this land

 I'm movin' on
Movin' on
You got me so down
Gonna leave this town
I'm a movin' on - Movin' on

Spent all my money on diamond rings
Furs and cars, all kinds of things
You were done, threw me away
That's alright momma gonna have my day

I'm movin' on
Movin' on
You got me so down
Gonna leave this town
I'm a movin' on - Movin' on

CROSSOVER

She's gone
Packed her bags and left today
She's gone
Sold my soul down pains highway

Done crossed over
Crossed on over that line

Shook my hand
Instead of kissin' me good-bye
Shook my hand
Instead of kissin' me good-bye

Done crossed over
Crossed over that line

She's gone
Packed her bags and left today
She's gone
Sold my soul down pains highway

Done crossed over
Crossed over that line
Done crossed over
Crossed over that line

PHILOSOPHICAL SAYINGS

&

DEFINITIONS

PHILOSOPHICAL SAYINGS

- Your sincerity is my inspiration.

- Let your money work for you.

- I'm not a genius but I play one on TV.

- Drink up and be somebody.

- You've heard the saying, 'Someone messed up so bad, they should be run out of town,' I've messed up so bad, I should be run out of the universe.

- See you later, only if I'm lucky.

- It could be worse, I could be married again.

- Someone once came up to me (looking upon me because of my spiritual background and the roads I've whored), "Give me your best advice." And I said, "The best advice is no vice at all."

- Something from nothing is something.

- When cooking, one has to talk to the food.

- When you fall in love with someone for who they are, for God's, sake don't try to change them.

- To lie in clover, and search for, and finally find a four-leaf… is one of life's greatest pleasures.

DEFINITIONS

- Kin-a : short for fuckin' alright
- Idgemo : (idge as in fridge) one stupid, dumbass person
- Buttmunch : enough said
- Condominium : man's monolith to madness
- Squatnot : a small, idgemo
- Tongue Boner : hard tongue (after spotting a good lookin' female carbon unit)

HICCUPS

Since the dawn of time, the hiccups have plagued man. Centuries and centuries have rolled by and man has never been able to get rid of the hiccups. Except through old wives tales like drinking water out of a cup with a paper towel over it, or bending over and drinking upside down, or holding your breathe while walking in a circle backwards (no, that's to get rid of a headache). Anyway, while I was growing up my parents used to tell me that when I had the hiccups I was growing. Hiccups make you grow.

Well a few years back, I got a bad case of the hiccups and I decided that I had had enough. So, I stumbled across a cure for the hiccups, which is guaranteed to work! Or your money back!

Step one: Take a deep breathe and hold it as long as you can without swallowing. Then exhale slowly through your mouth.

Step two: Repeat step one.

Step three: Repeat step two.

Step four: Now on your fourth time of inhaling as deep as you can, hold your breath as long as you can, without swallowing. You cannot swallow at any time during this process. So, holding your breath as long as possible slowly let it out through your nose. Do not swallow. Let it out

157

easy; slowly take a breath, without swallowing! Swallowing will make the hiccups start all over again, as well as someone making you laugh (I suggest going to a room by yourself).

Now slowly swallow your spit without laughing. And relax. Count to a hundred and breathe. Trust me, it works!

A MEMBRANTH

Written by: Megan Strickland

(This poem was written for school and presented on the one year anniversary of September 11)

United we stand
That was the motto we had.
So many lives claimed
Not just one man to blame.
Ground zero today
As al-Queda screamed hooray.
They swallowed our children, our women and men
And suckled away life in the rubble of tin.
Some say it made us stronger
Unfortunately for others there will be no tomorrow.
As we look upon that day many eyes fill with tears
While we try to rebuild and prepare for the years.
Flights now seem so rare
Thoughts of the innocent too hard to bare.
Whole families killed in the blink of an eye
Our men over there to make sure it's more than a tie.
Why all the suffering, the pain, and the hate?
When we catch Bin Laden we'll set him a date.
For whose who escaped, who ran, and who crawled
Poor victims at work caught up in the brawl.
So let us be silent and give them a membranth
For all those who died on September eleventh.

Acknowledgments

- **Dean Koontz**- permission for quotation
- **Cindy Vallar**- information for pirate story
- **Brother K.W.**- Impresario
- **Megan Strickland**- transcribing, spell check, editing, format and presentation of book
- **Tisha Strickland**- ideas (forgotten by dad) for book
- **Joe Gilchrist, Pat McClellan, the Managers, the Secretaries, the Maintenance Crew, Customer Service Staff, Kitchen Staff, Bartenders and Waitresses, Musicians, and especially all the customers that come out to the Flora-Bama to help support the music and good times**- I am acknowledging all these people for their spirit, love of life, and hard work.